MW00635659

From the Desk of the
ATTORNEY GENERAL

A Memoir

From the Desk of the ATTORNEY GENERAL

A Memoir

David M. Louie

© 2021 David M. Louie

All rights reserved. No part of this publication may be reproduced, stored in a retrieval system, or transmitted in any form or by any means, electronic, mechanical, photocopying, recording or otherwise, without the prior permission of the publisher.

ISBN 978-1-948011-56-3

Library of Congress Control Number: 2021910851

A portion of the proceeds from sales of this book will go to support the National Asian Pacific American Bar Association Law Foundation, to promote the development, advancement, leadership and public service of Asian Americans, Native Hawaiians and Pacific Islanders in the legal profession.

Design and production by Angela Wu-Ki

Legacy Isle Publishing
1000 Bishop St., Suite 806
Honolulu, HI 96813
www.legacyislepublishing.net
info@legacyislepublishing.net

Printed in Korea

CONTENTS

PREFACE

The first thing I noticed when I walked into my new office as attorney general was the desk. It was gigantic. Eight feet long and four feet across, it had an unusual design of intricate woodwork and brass hardware that said *old school*. It was not hard to notice that the desk had seen better days. It was slightly warped, the brass plates tarnished, portions of the desk missing or replaced with nontraditional materials, and not with care. It was finished in a dark rosewood color dulled with age, but there were places where the reddish paint had been chipped away, revealing the golden brown hues of koa, a hardwood endemic to Hawaiʻi and prized for its beauty. Koa furniture pieces have long been heirlooms in Hawaiʻi. This was obviously a historic desk.

I consulted Irving Jenkins, who wrote the seminal book *Hawaiian Furniture and Hawaii's Cabinetmakers*, and learned that this was probably the first of a series of thirteen desks used in government and made by Hawaiʻi craftsmen beginning in 1869, at the time of the Hawaiian monarchy. The governor, chief justice and director of public safety all had similar desks. Legendary surfer Duke Kahanamoku had used such a desk when he was sheriff of Honolulu.

What important papers, legislation and policies had been written on it? What discussions and decisions about the pressing issues of the day had been held around it? I once visited the Smithsonian National Museum of American History in Washington, DC, and marveled at the plain but historic table and chairs from Appomattox, where General Ulysses S. Grant and General Robert E. Lee sat to negotiate the surrender of the Confederacy and end the Civil War. To me, the desk was similarly imbued with the events it had seen and deserved to be restored to a fitting state for the events and decisions yet to come.

But getting the job done was not that easy. Government procurement policies required us to get bids, but the refinishers we contacted did not even bid. "Too old, too rare." Finally, Jenkins introduced me to Thor Minnick, a conservator who specialized in dealing with museum-quality pieces. Conservation requires specialized knowledge of chemistry, materials and historic techniques. Minnick took almost a year to restore the desk to its former glory, straightening the warp and replacing broken and missing parts. He stripped off the rosewood paint to reveal the original koa and finished it with an old-school French polish technique, applying many coats of shellac and hand rubbing them over and over again to achieve a lustrous finish.

When the desk was restored, I shared it with the public at the 2013 Hawai'i Forest Industry Association's annual Hawai'i's Woodshow, along with exhibiting some *'umeke* (Hawaiian bowls) I made using Island woods such as koa, mango and milo. It's funny, but over the years I have gotten many more comments and questions about my pastime as a woodturner and the restoration of the desk than about my work as attorney general. I think this is because the experiences of woodworkers are more relatable to the average person than the experience of being a government official.

Many people do not understand what public officials do or how government works. For them, government is a mystery in a foreign language, a black box, with incomprehensible processes. Some think this important institution is irretrievably screwed up and dysfunctional. Before I became attorney general, I occasionally wondered myself, given my limited experience with government. Serving four years as attorney general gave me a window into this world that changed my perspective and gave me a deep appreciation of the enduring value of our system of government.

Restoring the desk paralleled my own journey of discovery and education about our government. Starting with a blind leap of faith into the position, I got a rare front row seat to see how the sausage of government is made. Like the desk, I found an institutional process crafted long ago that is sometimes obscure, but that still functions, sometimes well, sometimes not so well, to live up to the lofty ideals of the Declaration of Independence and our federal and state constitutions. Like the restoration, I got to see beneath the surface and observe the actions, motivations and enthusiasm of the many hardworking people who make things happen in government. As I watched the desk being transformed, I also changed my perspective of government.

My seat at the desk gave me the opportunity to help move Hawaiʻi forward on some of the major issues of the day. Legalizing same-sex marriage, settling thirty-year-old claims by Native Hawaiians as well as defending Hawaiian rights at the US Supreme Court, enforcing criminal laws, protecting consumers and protecting the environment were just some of the wide-ranging issues we tackled on my watch. Along the way, I learned a lot about people, as well as myself, and it made me a better lawyer and a better person. It certainly changed the way I thought about government, politics and the law.

This book is a recap of my brief but intense four years in state government, the experiences and adventures I had, the trials and challenges I faced and the lessons I learned. My purpose is to give you a look behind the curtain at the position of attorney general and the broad scope of fascinating issues that I had the opportunity to address to try and make a difference. Being attorney general was the best job I ever had. Best. Job. Ever. I hope you enjoy my story. ❦

| 1 |

Someone's Future to Decide

In December 2010 I was a civil litigation lawyer in Honolulu. One day I was managing a law firm, representing clients in court, solving problems and fighting over money (which is generally what civil litigation lawyers do), and the very next day I was nominated by the newly elected governor, Neil Abercrombie, to be Hawai'i's attorney general. It was the equivalent of taking a high-speed elevator to the penthouse executive floor.

As a private attorney, I was simply a name on the door of the ninth floor in a building. Then that high-speed elevator took me to places where I was helping to advise the governor, his cabinet and the legislature, serving as the public face of law enforcement, opining as to the handling of legal and policy aspects of various major decisions for the State of Hawai'i and appearing on TV and on the front page of newspapers. It was a sudden and dramatic rise to the "room where it happens" in Hawai'i's state government. It was an unparalleled experience to participate in the process of governing, see who the players were on both the local and national stages, how they worked, who they were as politicians, entrepreneurs, goal-oriented doers, power-hungry grabbers—and people.

My tenure as attorney general started off fast. I was introduced to the public in a press conference by Gov. Abercrombie and got ready to take on the job. I was about to run the largest law firm in Hawai'i, with 185 attorneys, several hundred staff, a $70 million annual budget and the responsibility to provide legal counsel to everyone who worked for the State, from the governor to the guys sweeping up debris in the streets. The department handled legal matters ranging from constitutional questions to tax matters, environmental matters to labor disputes, land use issues to criminal law. You name it, we did it. It was a steep learning curve.

But the learning curve got even steeper the moment I got sworn in a few weeks after being nominated. In the first week on the job, I learned how fast-paced this life was, how high the stakes were, and how serious the human consequences could be.

Only minutes after I signed the oath of office and formally became the attorney general, Russell Suzuki, the first deputy attorney general, said that he and Chris Young, the supervisor of the Criminal Justice Division, needed to talk to me privately. Behind closed doors, they let me know that allegations of unethical and possibly illegal conduct had been made against two of the governor's cabinet nominees who had yet to be confirmed. Holy cow! I was only on the job a few minutes, and now we were going to make some decisions affecting the lives of two high-profile people.

For the past few weeks, I had been meeting with other cabinet nominees, getting to know them, forging alliances to work together on the governor's New Day agenda, and creating an atmosphere of cooperation. The attorney general advises, counsels and represents all of the departments, so there is a need for a close working relationship between the attorney general and the department directors. Developing trust, camaraderie and personal communication was important.

How would these accusations affect the governor, myself and my relations with the cabinet members? Whether the matters became public the next day or many months later, they were serious enough that they would likely be on the front page of the newspaper, above the fold, as well as on TV. It would be a matter of public interest and sensationalized for the voracious news cycle of gotcha. If the news appeared true, the governor's and my judgment would come into question. Regardless of truth or falsity, the questions would be "Had the cabinet nominee received special treatment, what did the governor know, and when did he know it?" If the allegations were substantial, the governor would have to defend both the person and his own actions in deciding to go forward with the appointment. Government appointees these days are like Caesar's wife; they must be above reproach.

Yet it was important to consider the effect that taking action would have on a potentially innocent person. The governor's cabinet nominees had already been publicly announced, so their backgrounds, achievements and fitness for the position were already being evaluated. Taking action to remove them from consideration would instantly start a cycle of questions about the reasons behind the action and what hidden secrets existed. The public scrutiny and the fallout for them and their families might be considerable.

There is really only one way forward in such a situation. Determine how much time you have, get the best information available, and then make a decision. I immediately informed the governor of the potential allegations, how serious they were, what we were doing to investigate, and how long we planned to take to make a recommendation.

The difference between the practice of law as a private lawyer and the practice of being attorney general was made starkly clear by these matters. In litigation, there is a deliberate and sometimes slow process, whether criminal or civil matters are involved. Where important rights or money are at issue, the accused defendant has a right to take sufficient time to find out the facts, prepare defenses and be thoroughly ready before facing a decision maker in the form of a judge or jury.

Not so in the world of government affairs and a voracious news cycle. The luxury of having perfect information to make a decision does not exist. Business, government, political and social environments move at the speed of thought. There is never enough time to get all the facts, since the cycle moves too quickly and can pass you by.

The first question always was, "How much time do we have?" Often the timetable is not within your control. Some decisions are hour or day decisions, others can take weeks or months. Some decisions don't necessarily have to be made. I remember a phrase from a book by Dick Francis, *The Edge*, which said, "Thought before action, if you've got time." I love this quote, because the question always is, "Can you think about what you're doing before action is required?"

One thing I always appreciated about making decisions in the attorney general world was that we could convene the best minds in the department to help with thinking and analysis. In private practice as an attorney, there were always economic constraints. Who's going to pay for all of those bodies and brainpower? Not so at the department of the attorney general. Depending on the importance of the issue, we could get the necessary help and analysis, because getting the right answer was most important. Of course, we could not be unreasonable as to the resources we used, but the determining factor was the importance of the issue, not the economics.

So how were decisions made? The decision tree would vary depending upon the issue or problem presented. What were the facts? What was known and unknown? What did the constitution or laws require? Were there prior court decisions or State policies or precedents? Were there general values and principles that needed to be upheld? What was the right thing to do? As long as we could consider all the relevant factors, understand what the constitution and the law required, and try to do the right thing, then I was comfortable with the decisions we made, even though we could be second-guessed.

In the case of these two investigations, we had less than a week to conclude them and make decisions. The timetable was largely driven by the fact that the cabinet nominees were coming up for Senate confirmation hearings. We did not want to have the Senate go forward with a committee hearing before the matters were fully vetted.

The first appointee I had to look at was the governor's nominee for the director of health, who would head one of the largest departments in state government, with control over a giant budget, policies and procedures affecting everyone in Hawai'i.

I was informed that a qui tam claim had been made against the nominee. A qui tam claim is potentially very serious. It is an accusation that false claims for government money have been made, which is illegal. The laws protect government from being deceived by parties who make false claims. They give an incentive to whistleblowers to come forward by giving them a percentage of any recovery, just like a contingency fee.

Qui tam claims are initially filed under seal and not made public for possibly months or years. This allows the government to investigate the claim without tipping off the possible wrongdoer to avoid them taking steps to cover their tracks or destroy evidence. Once a qui tam lawsuit is filed by a private party, the government has a certain amount of time to decide whether they will take over the prosecution. If the government decides to take over and prosecute, the whistleblower will share in the proceeds, but at a lesser rate. If the government decides not to do so, the whistleblower can get a bigger piece of the pie, if they win.

Someone had filed a false claims act lawsuit against the director of health nominee, claiming that he had been involved in a fraudulent billing scheme involving government contracts. The alleged fraud involved hundreds of thousands of dollars, multiple transactions over an extended period of time and written guidelines that could not easily be ignored. Although the investigation was still preliminary, the allegations were that the nominee was possibly central to the scheme as the head of the company doing the billing—in a clear position to have known of the fraud.

Although the complaint was filed under seal and still confidential, this created a situation where the matter could and would likely become public in the future, with the potential to embarrass everyone. When, not if, the lawsuit became public, there would be predictable, hard questions for the governor and the attorney general. If the nominee had been confirmed, the inquiry would be even more pointed. Did the governor and attorney general know of these claims when this individual was nominated for a position as the head of one of the most powerful and critical departments? Were these claims investigated before the nominee was pushed forward or confirmed? Were you just ignorant, or complicit? Were you stupid or corrupt? We needed to know whether the claims had any merit whatsoever.

I soon found out that the qui tam claims had been filed by former attorney general Margery Bronster. She had served as AG under Gov. Ben Cayetano and had been involved in the prosecution of claims for malfeasance and breach of trust by the Bishop Estate trustees—some of the most powerful people in Hawaiʻi in their oversight roles with the Bernice Pauahi Bishop Trust for the benefit of the Kamehameha Schools. Bronster could not get confirmed for a second term as attorney general because of the political fallout from the lawsuits, but she was well regarded and was no fly-by-night attorney. As a former attorney general of the State, she had credibility and clout. This was obviously a serious matter, not to be dismissed lightly.

I met with Bronster, whom I personally had worked with on cases, to find out what information and evidence she had. Bronster told me that she represented a whistleblower, and that the nominee was the head of a medical group that had submitted numerous billings for medical services to the State that violated Medicaid regulations and thus were fraudulent. The claims were for hundreds of thousands of dollars. I asked if the nominee was perhaps only a peripheral figure or incidental defendant. No, she said. He was the head of the medical group and most likely would have had knowledge of the medical billing practices. Moreover, Bronster shared copies of some of the medical billings with me, and I personally reviewed them. It appeared to me that there were approximately a thousand billings that had been submitted that appeared to be signed by the nominee. Even if the nominee had a good and compelling explanation, the evidence looked quite convincing and could be spun negatively against both him and the governor, if the governor chose to stand behind him.

At the same time as we were conducting the director of health nominee investigation, I also had to conduct an investigation of Bruce Coppa, the appointee to be the comptroller, the head of the Department of Accounting and General Services. An allegation had been made that Coppa was an employee or agent of a company that had improperly been awarded a government contract by the Department of Transportation (DOT). While the Coppa investigation was on a smaller scale than the Department of Health investigation, it also involved government contracting, procurement and the possible misuse of government funds.

Because there was no evidence, only an allegation, I met with Coppa and asked him directly about his relationship with the DOT official, the government contract in question and whether he had personally profited from the transaction. This was the first time I had met Coppa. He was quite forthright and said that he had known of the proposed contract, had a passing relationship with the official, but that no deal had been made, no contract had been signed; he had received nothing. Coppa showed me emails and records that nothing had happened.

Within a few days I met with the governor, along with first deputy Suzuki, to explain the results of our investigations. The governor queried us at length, and we explored all possible outcomes. After deliberation, the governor made a decision. Coppa would proceed forward, but the nominee for director of health would not.

That night, the governor had to meet with both men to discuss what was going to happen, because there was a meeting of the prospective cabinet the very next day to discuss the governor's agenda, vision and plans. Since Coppa was going forward, he would be at the meeting. But the director of health nominee would not, and I would need to explain to the cabinet, in vague but final terms, that his nomination was being withdrawn.

Unfortunately, because the qui tam suit was still sealed and confidential, the governor could not even tell the director of health nominee the reason the nomination was being withdrawn. He could only be told that something had arisen in the investigation of his background, and that he was out. This was a personally gut-wrenching call for me, since it was clear that there might be idle speculation in the media and the nominee's reputation for character and integrity might take a very public hit.

Yet if no action was taken, the governor would be subject to a ticking time bomb that could go off at any time and imperil him as well as all of the good work that he planned to do. If the Senate had a confirmation hearing and the whistleblower came forward, the governor's judgment as well as that of the attorney general would be called into question. If the matter was not made public until after the nominee was confirmed, the problem would become infinitely worse. The judgment had to be made now because the alternative was worse.

The next day I showed up for the cabinet meeting at Washington Place, a historic mansion built in the mid-1800s, which had been the private residence of Queen Liliʻuokalani, the last queen of the Hawaiian kingdom, and for many years had served as both the living quarters for the governor and his family and a ceremonial venue for bill signings, receptions and parties. It is a historical residence with many museum-quality pieces of furniture, old memorabilia and historical artifacts; a graceful, lovely and fitting place for the new administration to begin discussing and implementing its agenda for the people of Hawaiʻi.

I was surprised to see that the director of health nominee was there. Had he not gotten the message? Did he not meet with the governor? Did he think that someone was kidding and he would get a last-minute reprieve? Beats me. I did not ask him. All I knew was that I was going to have to let everyone else know that he was out, and that I couldn't tell anyone, least of all him, the exact reasons why.

We had some meetings about the governor's New Day vision, platform and agenda. Then we went to lunch, where I found myself sitting next to Coppa. By chance, the director of health nominee sat almost directly across the table from us. As we were eating, Coppa launched into a discussion about how he had met with the governor the night before and had been told that he'd been investigated by the attorney general over possible improprieties in some government contract, but that he had been cleared. He went on and on, even though I tried to change the subject. The director of health nominee was listening to the whole discussion. Awkward!

Shortly thereafter, we resumed the meeting of the entire cabinet. After a few preliminary matters were handled, I stood up and let everyone know that unfortunately, the nomination for director of health was being withdrawn. Something had come up that I was not at liberty to discuss, but we wished him well in his future endeavors. I told the cabinet members there would be no explanations of this matter, and they should not speculate about the reasons for this action. The director of health nominee was sitting right in front. Double awkward!

The announcement was made publicly later that day. There was immediate speculation by the news media as to the reasons why. We had no comment. Because the person involved was well known in the community, there was much questioning from his supporters as to what he had done to have been so poorly treated, since no explanations were forthcoming. This was an unfortunate outcome, but it was necessary because the lawsuit was still under seal.

A couple of years later I learned that the qui tam lawsuit had become a matter of public record and both the federal government and the State had taken over the claims and proceeded against the nominee's medical group. The medical group denied the claims and fought them in court. The claims were later settled for hundreds of thousands of dollars, although there was no adjudication and no finding of wrongdoing on the part of the nominee.

This episode made clear to me how important appearances and perceptions could be in the political realm. Perception is reality, as they say. Although it was difficult to decide someone's future based upon the allegations in a lawsuit, they were serious enough, and the supporting evidence was substantial enough, that there was serious risk if the nomination went forward. Neither I nor the governor could take the chance that the claims against the director of health nominee might be true and taint the image of the governor.

I also realized the significant effects decisions could have on people's lives and reputations in the blink of an eye. Government is serious business. There is substantial money, time and effort being spent by lots of people in and out of government who are trying to make things happen, and when people get caught up in matters that have political consequences, their lives and reputations can be affected, both positively and negatively, in a heartbeat. Unfortunately, that is the risk that all of us must take if we want to make a contribution in the public sphere.

Dealing with these accusations was my initiation into how to approach decision-making on issues that had both legal and political consequences. When there are winners and losers, someone was always going to be unhappy or disappointed. But as long as I made my decisions based upon principled reasons, then I could live with myself and accept the consequences of my actions. I took no delight in having to tell the director of health nominee that he was out. But under the circumstances, it was the best decision for all involved.

The pace of decision-making in this episode had been fast and furious, and this was just my first week. It was apparent to me that this job might be a very fast ride indeed.

| 2 |

Buckle Up

One of the great things about the American dream is the idea that anyone can achieve anything, even become president of the US or obtain other high office. While the reality is much more complicated, it's also true that opportunity abounds and there are many paths forward for all of us. The path that led me to be the attorney general of Hawaiʻi was a meandering one, not direct or clear. The unexpected opportunity to serve as attorney general happened to intersect with who I was and what I was doing. While perhaps fortuitous, my background and experiences helped to prepare me for the challenges of serving.

On occasion, I have reflected (sometimes in amazement) on how I got to where I am. I owe much to the advantages and opportunities provided by my family. My family's story and background, like that of many Americans, is one of immigrants making their way forward by dint of hard work. My grandfather, Louie Loy, came to the United States in 1882 from a small village in rural southern China a few months before the passage of the Chinese Exclusion Act by the United States Congress, which shut the country's door to Chinese immigrants for more than sixty years. He learned English, became a merchant and ran a women's undergarments store. He was successful, made money and bought land, but he was swindled and lost his fortune. The family ended up living in Seattle's Chinatown, eking out a living.

Both of my parents set examples that led me to appreciate the importance of public service and doing things for the good of the community. My father, Paul Louie, was one of twelve children and was the first in his family to attend and graduate from college. He then went on to Harvard Divinity School and became a minister in the Presbyterian Church. After twenty years as a minister, influenced by the civil rights struggles of Blacks and other minorities in the 1960s and his own experience working on Fair Housing initiatives, he decided to make a career change. In 1970 he joined the staff of the Los Angeles County Human Relations Commission to work with Asian American communities. He helped to establish a Teen Post and a public library branch in Chinatown, and he worked with Korean, Vietnamese and Cambodian immigrant communities in Los Angeles.

My mother, Emma Louie, grew up in San Francisco's Chinatown and became a nurse. She met and married my father when he moved to San Francisco. She worked in various hospital emergency rooms and intensive care units, then became a research assistant interviewing Chinese American patients for a cancer research project. Pursuing her pastime on how names developed, she authored *Chinese American Names: Tradition & Transition*, a scholarly book on how Chinese Americans adapted Chinese names to American naming customs.

I grew up in California. I attended public schools at a time when California's schools were some of the best in the nation. I attended Occidental College, and after graduation I didn't know what I wanted to do, so I spent a year doing odd jobs and working as an apprentice carpenter building homes, offices and freeways. It was hard, tiring, at times dangerous physical labor. Although the money was good, I saw no future and did not want to keep doing that work, so I decided to invest in my education and find another career. I went to law school at the University of California at Berkeley, now known as Berkeley Law.

While many people born in Hawai'i have left to pursue opportunities and careers on the mainland, I ended up doing the opposite. In my third year of law school, I arranged to work for a semester at a major Hawai'i law firm that later became Case & Lynch. The firm offered me a job as an associate and I accepted, thinking I would stay in Hawai'i just for a few years. But Hawai'i is such a wonderful place and I had good opportunities, so I stayed and thrived. Johanna, my wife, whom I met in law school, joined me in Honolulu, and we started a family with two children, Ryan and Jenna, and made Hawai'i our home.

For thirty plus years I was a trial lawyer doing civil litigation, working for private clients such as insurance companies, construction companies, businesses and individuals. I handled cases involving personal injuries, construction defects and commercial disputes. I became a partner at Case & Lynch, then left and co-founded the law firm of Roeca Louie & Hiraoka. I was the managing partner for about twenty years. I tried jury cases and worked closely with clients to solve and settle their legal problems.

Because Hawai'i has a relatively small legal community, the litigation law practice here has been more collegial and less combative than the practice in California and other large cities as reported to me by friends. While litigation lawyers in big cities on the mainland would likely not see the opposing lawyer again, and so could act like jerks with impunity, in Hawai'i the likelihood was that you would see the same lawyers over and over again, and your reputation would precede you. So litigation in Hawai'i has always been conducted with a lot more aloha than can be found on the mainland. I found it to be enjoyable and rewarding.

In hindsight, a litigation background proved to be very helpful in navigating the challenges of office. Politics and government involve competing interests and policies, so knowing how courts think is very helpful in evaluating such issues as they arise. Litigation requires understanding of process, persuasion, decision-making and conflict resolution, as well as leverage and dealing with adversaries.

I also had some experience with Hawai'i's government and institutions as president of the Hawaii State Bar Association (HSBA), chair of the State of Hawai'i Aloha Tower Development Corporation (charged with developing the waterfront next to downtown) and co-chair of the Hawai'i Supreme Court Rule 19 Committee on Judicial Performance (overseeing a program for lawyers to evaluate the performance of judges). These experiences gave me some familiarity with state government, how things worked and how decisions were made.

In 2010, I was happy. I had great clients, the firm was doing well, and we were having fun solving problems and making enough money. And then an opportunity came along that literally changed my life. I became the Hawai'i attorney general almost by accident. It was an opportunity that I initially passed up. But luckily for me, the opportunity came around again, and I took it.

In most states in the Union, the attorney general is chosen by the voters. Forty-three of the fifty states select their top legal officer by statewide election. In Hawai'i and four other states, the attorney general is appointed by the governor, just like the federal model where the president of the United States picks the United States attorney general.

Before 2010, I had dabbled in politics for many years—donating money here and there to support candidates, going to fundraisers and dinners, meeting with political figures every now and then. I had friends who were politically very active, although I was not. One of my old friends, William "Bill" Kaneko, was the campaign chair for Neil

Abercrombie in 2010. Kaneko had recruited me to assist in the campaign, so I had helped to campaign for Abercrombie.

Through Kaneko, I had met and talked with Abercrombie during the campaign and was impressed by his intellect, energy, wide-ranging grasp of many issues and his many decades of public service. He had served on the Honolulu City Council, was both a representative and a senator in the Hawaiʻi State Legislature and represented Hawaiʻi for seventeen years as a US House representative. He was known as a free-wheeling, iconoclastic and bright politician, with longish hair and an almost hippie-like appearance. He famously once wrote to a State Board of Education official with a text of just two words: "Fuck you." He was known for being combative and for taking on positions that were not always the most popular, but he was a very principled person. Just my kind of guy.

In August 2010, Abercrombie beat Mufi Hannemann to be the Democratic nominee for governor. Hawaiʻi is a solidly Democratic state, so it looked like Abercrombie would likely be elected governor in November 2010. Kaneko was serving as the head of the transition team, not to count the chickens before they hatched but to begin thinking about people who might serve in the cabinet so they would be ready if they won.

Governing is a team sport. A successful governor surrounds himself with competent, intelligent and practical people who can achieve and put his or her vision into practice. Because the four-year cycle of political life for a governor is very short to actually get things done, he or she needs to hit the ground running.

One day in September 2010, Kaneko asked me if I would be interested in applying to be the attorney general. At the time, I was happy in my practice as a lawyer, happy in my outside activities and not looking for a change. Most importantly, I felt responsible for the people in my law firm. Although I would not describe myself as indispensable, since no one ever is, I had helped build the firm, I was the managing partner, and I was bringing in my fair share of business. I had seen other law firms come and go when key members moved on to other pursuits, and I was concerned about what might happen to my law firm if I left. So I said, "No."

But I also volunteered to be on the transition team to select the attorney general, because I thought it was an important position and I personally knew many attorneys. The team reviewed a number of résumés and conducted interviews. I was fine with some of the candidates and thought they would be good as attorney general. But others on the transition team were not as satisfied. One of the candidates withdrew, and the position remained unfilled. The transition team was filling the other cabinet positions, Gov. Abercrombie was sworn into office at noon on the first Monday of December 2010, and there was still no attorney general. Time was getting short.

Kaneko and Kate Stanley, who were both on the transition team, came to see me and asked if I would reconsider applying for the attorney general position. I told them I would think about it. Over the intervening time that I had served on the transition team, I had begun to think this was something I might want to do. This was a rare chance to do interesting work that was radically different from my prior practice, that might allow me to make a difference and give back to the community.

But I was still worried about changing my life in a major way, leaving the comfortable confines of my law firm for the unknowns of government service and how this might affect my firm. I'm sure others have had similar concerns when faced with the possibility of substantial changes to their lives and careers. So I went to see a good friend, Alan Oshima, a successful lawyer who had left a prominent law firm bearing his name to become president of Hawaiian Telcom and later the president of Hawaiian Electric Company, two major institutions in Hawai'i. When Oshima left his law firm, it had broken up and the people had moved on. So I asked him what he thought about my concerns. He gave me some great advice.

Oshima told me that I should follow the best opportunity for me, that I did not owe others a future, and that each person in my firm would find their own level of success commensurate with their skills and talents. He said I should not live my life worrying about the consequences to others, since those can't be predicted and were not my responsibility. In short, he said to do what would be interesting to me and not worry about consequences to the firm, because those would be manageable. His advice set my mind at ease.

I also called the former attorneys general that I personally knew—Warren Price, Robert Marks and Margery Bronster—to ask their advice. They all told me it was a great job, I would never have such an opportunity again, and I should seek the job and not look back.

The next day, I told Kaneko and Stanley that I would apply. They told me that there was another candidate who was very qualified, whom I knew. It was another friend of mine who was a well-respected lawyer. I told them I would be fine with his selection, as he was a highly qualified individual with a great deal of character and integrity. They told me to get ready for interviews with the transition team and the governor.

The next few days were a whirlwind. I interviewed with the transition team, which I had been working with over the past month. I suppose I had some advantage, since I had seen the other candidates interview and had been thinking about the job—what it meant to the state government, what it meant to the people of Hawai'i and what it meant to me. I told my law partners, Art Roeca and Keith Hiraoka, that I was interviewing for the job and, if offered, would take it. I interviewed with the governor, and he offered me the job. I immediately accepted.

Gov. Abercrombie then held a press conference and introduced me as the next attorney general. My mom, brothers and sister came to Hawai'i for the press conference and announcement. I was pleased they could be present. My father had passed away a couple of years before, so he missed it. I was proud to be his son and to try and make a contribution to the people of Hawai'i. Now I had the opportunity to revisit some of the things I had thought about as a young lawyer.

When I went to law school, I thought about working to right wrongs, achieve social justice and help the downtrodden and the poor. I had grown up during the early years of the civil rights movement and had been inspired by how law and decisions from the United States Supreme Court could improve society and the lives of people. I wanted to be a trial lawyer, giving a stellar courtroom closing argument, like Louis Nizer or Clarence Darrow. I thought about how I could use knowledge of the law to fight discrimination, achieve equal opportunity and address problems of inequality. My father and my brother Stephen were both involved in working with Asian American immigrant communities, which could always use legal representation.

When I got out of law school, I thought about following a career as a community or government lawyer. But I decided that I wanted to learn the craft of lawyering and become as proficient and professional as possible. At the time, the conventional wisdom was that established law firms would provide better training and opportunities for trial experience, and I could learn from skilled professionals who had proven success. Of course, that is not necessarily true, and many great trial lawyers have honed their skills through other paths. But I did not realize that then. Besides, I had a job offer with a major private law firm, so I didn't look further.

After I started working, making money, getting experience and taking on more responsibilities, I got caught up in furthering my career as a lawyer. I also got caught up in the problems of my clients and how I could advance their interests. When I started a law firm with Art Roeca and Keith Hiraoka, I got caught up in the thousand and one things that make a law firm run—how to manage the firm, how to get more clients, how to make a buck and how to do this or that to advance my cases and the causes of my clients. I lost sight of some of the dreams that I had as a young man.

But my appointment to be the attorney general of Hawaiʻi was an opportunity for me to do some of those things I had thought about long ago. This was a moment of serendipity, of being in the right place at the right time. Muhammad Ali once said, "Service to others is the rent you pay for your room here on earth." This was an opportunity to give back, to repay the people of Hawaiʻi for the wonderful life the islands have given me and my family, to be part of something with a larger meaning and purpose than my law firm and clients. It was also an opportunity to change my practice, learn new skills, meet new people and see things from a different perspective. It was time to pay the rent.

Public service is a noble pursuit. My father spent his entire life in the service of others, first as a minister, then as a human relations consultant for Los Angeles County. He participated in many initiatives to help poor and immigrant Asian American communities. Although my father had passed away a few years before, I thought about him as I pursued this position.

Being appointed attorney general meant that there was great power and authority that was being entrusted to me. Were my hands big enough to hold it? Would I rise to the occasion? Could I make positive things happen, be a force for good? I had concerns, because it would be a steep learning curve and I had not undertaken such a position and such a responsibility previously. But I had years of experience as a lawyer. I had confidence in myself, and I had confidence in the people around me. I took the leap, went forward and did my best to do what I thought was right, and tried to constantly learn as much as possible to master the job as I went along.

I was given an extraordinary opportunity to contribute as well as learn. What I found was that public service and working with others to improve our communities is tremendously rewarding and educational. I hope that anyone who cares about our shared future will step forward and do the same. Don't wait. While there are no set paths to becoming attorney general, there are abundant opportunities to serve in both elective and appointive capacities, as government relies upon many people voluntarily serving on boards and commissions, as well as employees, to make a contribution. There are many ways for people in both the private and public sectors to participate. Having experience in government processes and institutions is beneficial, but not necessary, to make a difference, participate and do some good. ❦

| 3 |

Get a Dog

Once I took this job, I had a lot to learn. New rules, new procedures, new people, new ways of looking at the world. I thought I was sufficiently prepared with thirty years as a trial lawyer and some experience in government. But this was not just any old legal job in state government. This was the top job at the intersection of law, government and politics. It was the big leagues, the deep end of the pool. While I had a lot of experience in law, I had only limited experience in politics and government. I quickly had to learn how to maneuver in those worlds. There were trials and tribulations to come, traps for the unwary and pitfalls that needed to be avoided. Talk about on-the-job training.

Litigation and law are processes that have evolved over centuries to resolve disputes and conflict in a civilized manner. There are rules, lots of rules, stylized procedures that lawyers have to observe while fighting in court. Trial lawyers can push the boundaries of those rules, but at the end of the day, there is a judge who will make a decision, like a referee in a boxing ring. Although government also has rules, politics has very few. The difference between fighting in court as a lawyer and political fighting is like the difference between a boxing match with a referee and a street brawl outside a bar. As I started to carry out my duties, I got an education in politics, people and power.

I have always thought of politics and government as a sumo wrestling match. Because of the large Japanese American population in Hawaiʻi and the large numbers of Japanese tourists who come to Hawaiʻi, sumo wrestling used to be regularly on TV in the 1970s. Sumo is a contest of very large, half-naked men pushing and shoving each other to force the other out of the ring, to establish dominance, power and authority. Politics and government are similar. There are many half-naked and sometimes fully naked vested interests and people playing in the arena, pushing and shoving each other, vying for money, power and influence. Government decisions, legislation and regulations often directly affect the lives and fortunes of many people. The stakes are high.

The attorney general has a significant role in the business of government. Laws, processes and procedures have to be followed in order for government actions and legislation to be valid and effective. The advice of the attorney general is often needed by government agencies to make sure they are acting within the law, in order to accomplish their goals. Deputy attorneys general assist some clients by drafting or rewriting legislation. Sometimes people wanted the cooperation of the attorney general or just wanted to check a box. Sometimes we were viewed by the client as an obstacle. Other times they wanted the attorney general to rubber-stamp their plans so they could tout such approval, especially in controversial situations. Then, if people criticized their plan, they could blame the attorney general.

Most of the legislators I dealt with were straightforward in simply wanting to get good legal advice and guidance to understand the law and figure out how to legally accomplish their goals. Others wanted to know how to bend the law to their purposes. A few legislators sought to impress upon me that I was supposed to be their attorney, and that I needed to always take their side and act in their best interests. Of course, those few were wrong. The attorney general serves the entire State and, most importantly, the people of Hawai'i. In other words, the attorney general is the attorney for the institution of the State, not just a lawyer for individual legislators, cabinet members or officials. While I had a duty to listen and provide them with advice and counsel, I had no obligation to simply do their bidding or to be their legal errand boy. But that's the way some of them saw it.

I thought I had sufficient preparation for this environment, as litigation taught me to watch out for the tactics of adversaries. I had learned long ago to trust but verify, to accept at face value until proven wrong, but always, always cut the cards. You hope for the best in people, but you plan for the worst. Still, I was a little surprised when attempts were made by people, who otherwise seemed friendly, to set up the attorney general to take a fall.

A few months into the job, during my first legislative session, I was summoned to a meeting with two state senators a few days before a deadline for third reading and final approval of bills in the Senate. They handed me a draft bill that was a classic "gut-and-replace" bill. Gut and replace is a legislative tactic that has often been criticized by proponents of transparency in government. The process involves taking a bill with a generic title that has already passed through two of the required three readings, gutting its contents and replacing it with something radically different, so the new bill can get approved by only having to go through one final reading and vote.

The draft gut-and-replace bill that was handed to me would have legalized gambling in Hawai'i. Gambling has been a contentious issue at the Hawai'i legislature for decades. So many people from Hawai'i regularly travel to Las Vegas to gamble that it is referred to as "the ninth island." There have been numerous and serious efforts for decades to legalize gambling in some form or another in Hawai'i, but the Catholic Church and other anti-gambling forces have successfully blocked those efforts. The strategy was clever, daring and calculated to avoid contentious committee hearings and the opposition of anti-gambling community groups. Hawai'i was having a fiscal crisis and was financially underwater by about $500 million. As will be described later, Gov. Abercrombie was looking for money anywhere he could. The senators were trying to use this fiscal crisis to accomplish a goal that had been thwarted for many years. The senators just wanted me, as attorney general, to bless it. I surmised that they wanted the cover of the attorney general so they could blame me when the predictable firestorm of opposition would erupt. I politely told them I would study it, then declined to give them the blessing they sought, since such a major change in policy should not be implemented in this fashion.

On another occasion, a prominent state senator asked my office to help revise the State's ethics laws. The ethics laws are quite robust and were being interpreted by the Ethics Commission to severely restrict government employees, including legislators, from receiving any gifts or meals greater than a $25 "gift of aloha." Years before, politicians had freely received expensive meals, trips and golf outings. Some politicians did not feel that taking such favors meant that they were corrupt, so they bristled at the restrictions. We drafted a bill that modestly relaxed the ethics rules on meals. But the senator wanted more and drafted a bill that eviscerated the rules to allow legislators to accept unlimited amounts of food and drink, even a container truck full of steaks, produce and liquor, without breaking the laws.

I thought this was audacious and said we would not support it. But the real audacity was yet to come. Someone leaked the senator's bill, and when the press called, the senator's office claimed the attorney general had drafted it. The press called us to confirm. Was this true? Would we take the blame for the client? Absolutely not! I was disappointed but not surprised. I had learned from many years of litigation that silence is often taken as assent, so if you are silent in the face of a falsehood, the perception can become the reality. We immediately called the senator's office and told them to take credit for the bad bill, or we would let the press know the full story. The senator's office retracted their claim and admitted they had drafted it. The bill predictably died. This episode reminded me that I had to watch out, even from those we served.

Because the stakes are high, and money, power and prestige are on the line, the world of politics and government can be a rough-and-tumble environment. Under these circumstances, it is no surprise that people would try to get their way by doing and saying things that might be considered questionable or over the line. When politicians are trying to avoid blame or obtain a result, sometimes they do not care if they act in a manner that would not be countenanced by people of goodwill or among friends. That is simply the political world. As President Harry S. Truman famously said, "If you want a friend in Washington, get a dog." As I went forward, I realized that a number of my experiences were really just politics as usual.

Confirmation

There are many tests that each of us face in our lives, some more onerous or fraught with peril than others. This is especially true in the legislature with respect to cabinet members and appointees. Various politicians and lobbyists are always trying to accomplish their goals or agendas, whether large or small. They are always doing things for their reasons, not your reasons. When they meet a new appointee, sometimes they will push or try and test you to see what you are made of, whether you will acquiesce to their assertion of power, whether you can be pushed around, whether you will stand up. My first test came with Clayton Hee, chair of the Senate Judiciary Committee.

Senator Hee was a longtime legislator with a reputation as an intelligent and clever bully who would push his weight around to achieve his goals. He was more feared than liked, but he had been involved in many progressive causes, had done some good things and was a friend of the governor. As Judiciary chair, Hee was responsible for holding my confirmation hearing, as well as hearing many of the bills affecting the attorney general and law enforcement. Hee could thus affect my confirmation, and if I passed that hurdle, also my function and effectiveness as attorney general.

I was sworn in as attorney general earlier than I had planned, because under the law I had to take the oath of office before the legislative session began in order to provisionally serve as the attorney general, subject to Senate confirmation. If I was sworn in after the session began, I could not do the job until I was actually confirmed by the full Senate. I had planned to take much more time to wind down my private law practice. But if I waited, Hee could delay my confirmation, and thus my ability to do the job, for months. Because of his reputation, I thought he might try to leverage me, so it was untenable to wait. Welcome to politics. I took the oath a few days before the session began.

This was only the prelude to a run-in with Hee that was a lot more complicated. One of the deputy attorneys general who was a friend of Hee told me that the senator wanted him to be temporarily reassigned by the attorney general to the senator's office for the full duration of the legislative session. A few days later, Charlie Toguchi, one of the governor's close confidants in charge of helping me get confirmed, took me to visit various senators. We met with Hee, but Hee did not mention this request for reassignment in front of Toguchi. Instead, later that day Hee called me to meet with him privately, and behind closed doors he told me what he wanted.

The request by Senator Hee was not without precedent, but it was also not normal and was really a demand. Hee told me that I needed to reassign this deputy to him for his sole use during the session. I asked if he would pay the deputy's salary. He said no, since he did not have a budget for that; that was my problem, not his. It was made clear to me that if I did not comply with this demand, things might go badly with my confirmation, as well as with various bills and initiatives that might come before him. I told him I would consider his request. He was not happy about any delay and made it clear that there was only one acceptable answer.

As it turned out, I was only a small part of a power play that Hee was attempting to engineer in the Senate. As I inquired, I learned that the Senate leadership did not want senators making demands on departments and agencies to loan them staff. Senate president Shan Tsutsui told me that this was a matter of internal Senate policies and procedures, and that I should not honor Hee's request. Tsutsui was considering a plan of having Senate leadership prohibit such requests and limit senators to their normal staff allotments. Senate leadership was concerned that this practice, which had been utilized occasionally in the past, was a possible vehicle for abuse, with an appearance of quid pro quo favors for confirmation of appointees and legislative bills. Notwithstanding this sentiment, it appeared that Hee wanted to amass additional staffers outside of their control. I learned that Senator Hee had also made a similar demand upon the chief justice of the Hawai'i Supreme Court.

I consulted with the governor's team. Toguchi felt that the request should be honored, since there were many initiatives the governor wanted to get through the legislature, and he was counting on Senator Hee's help. Since this was the governor's first year in office, the legislature was taking the measure of the governor and was pushing its own agendas and ideas, so every bit of support was important.

How to negotiate this dilemma? Would giving in to the demand be a fatal sign of weakness, of knuckling under to a bully, or simply going along to get along, especially in light of past precedent? How would this affect my confirmation and the governor's initiatives? I was uncertain as to the proper course of action.

The weekend came and I continued to ponder this. The senator had demanded an answer by Tuesday. I thought about this long and hard, and on Sunday I told Toguchi that I would probably agree, in order to advance the governor's initiatives and because the practice had been followed in the past. Toguchi went to see Hee for dinner that night and delivered the message that I would agree.

On Monday, I called Senate president Tsutsui and let him know that I was reluctantly going to agree to Hee's demand, because there was precedent and it would further the governor's initiatives, but that if he could finesse the situation and tell the senator no as a Senate procedural matter, I would be happy with that. I then scheduled a meeting with Hee for Tuesday morning at 10 a.m.

On Tuesday at 9 a.m., as I was getting ready to go see Hee, I got a call from Tsutsui. Senate leadership had discussed the matter and Senate vice president Donna Kim had raised the question of whether I was giving in to this demand just to get confirmed; and if so, this raised a question of what else I would be willing to sacrifice to further my own personal agenda. Tsutsui did not say whether Senate leadership was going to take any action to block Hee's demand. He told me that regardless of how the

Senate might enforce its own internal rules, if I agreed to the request, Kim had said she would make this an issue at my confirmation. Great. I was now a football in play between Hee and Senate leadership, and I was going to be made an example of no matter which way I turned. Pick your poison.

However, the situation was now clarified. If Kim thought that agreeing to Hee's demand looked like caving in and selling my position, then others might think the same way. I could not allow that if I was going to serve as attorney general. It was clear that regardless of what rationales or precedent might exist, I would now have to refuse Hee's demand and take whatever lumps might come my way.

I walked up to the Capitol Building to deliver my message and take my medicine. The meeting with Hee did not go well. He welcomed me into his office expecting me to say yes. It was an unpleasant surprise for me to tell him no, and that the reason was that I had been told by Senate leadership that if I agreed it would affect my confirmation. He was furious. The menace and threat in his voice was clear and unmistakable. I had crossed a line and refused an offer that I should not have refused. He kicked me out of his office.

For the next several months, I was frozen out. Hee would not meet with me to discuss any legislative bills and would not schedule a hearing for my confirmation. The governor's team asked him to schedule a confirmation hearing, but he refused. It was not until shortly before the end of the legislative session that I learned that the governor and Tsutsui had intervened and told Hee that if he didn't schedule the confirmation hearing, the Senate leadership would yank the matter from his committee. Under that pressure, Hee finally relented and scheduled a hearing.

The delay of several months turned out to be a blessing in disguise. Over the course of the several months from January to the end of April, I had a chance to learn the job and familiarize myself with many of the issues the attorney general is expected to know. I had the opportunity to get prepared. If I had gone before the Senate Judiciary Committee early in the legislative session, I would not have known as much, not been familiar with the law, policies, protocols and procedures, and would have been forced to admit my ignorance regarding many of the constitutional, administrative, criminal and civil issues that come before the attorney general. Other nominees have floundered and been rejected when they displayed substantial ignorance of the issues relating to their jobs. The questioning in the committee hearing was long and detailed, and it strayed into many esoteric and subtle issues, but because I had been learning on the job, I was comfortable discussing all of them. I was finally passed out of the Judiciary Committee and confirmed by the full Senate, just prior to the end of the legislative session.

Confirmation had been unexpectedly more difficult and fraught than I had imagined it would be. I had naively thought at the beginning that it would simply be based on my qualifications, experience and ability to serve. But as with many things in the world of politics and government, those were only some of the factors involved, and in my case, apparently not the most important ones. Nominees for government positions have been and will continue to be political footballs at times, when objectives or goals other than simply vetting qualifications become part of the equation. Sometimes those goals might be political or ideological; sometimes they might be personal and petty. It is the gauntlet that nominees must run to serve. I was glad that I had made it through.

The Hawai'i Health Connector

Sometimes important initiatives can be made unnecessarily complicated and hang in the balance because of foolish behavior. A particularly tense episode occurred while we were in the middle of setting up the Hawai'i Health Connector as part of the Affordable Care Act (ACA), the national health plan initiated by President Barack Obama and passed by Congress. The ACA was important legislation that, among other things, resulted in providing health insurance to tens of millions of uninsured people and preventing insurers from refusing to cover preexisting medical conditions. The Connector was an entity charged with creating an online marketplace where uninsured individuals could get affordable health insurance plans. The stakes were high because the ACA was controversial and there were tens of thousands of medically uninsured people in Hawai'i.

The State had chosen to take tens of millions of dollars from the federal government to set up the Connector and create an online marketplace for Hawai'i, rather than letting the federal government do it. Hawai'i had an overriding concern that its existing Prepaid Health Care laws remain fully in effect and not be negatively impacted by the ACA. Hawai'i's health care laws are some of the best in the nation, mandating employer funding of health care benefits at levels substantially better than the ACA. There was significant concern that Hawai'i's laws might be jeopardized if the federal government set up the system instead of the State.

The attorney general was tasked with assisting the Department of Health (DOH) to get the proper contracts for the sharing of personal medical information between individuals, the Connector, state agencies and insurance companies. The documentation was complicated because we were dealing with sensitive medical information and complex privacy laws.

As negotiations were proceeding, the deputy attorney general supervisor in charge of interfacing with the Connector kept me apprised. There was a critical deadline approaching to get an agreement signed between the DOH and the Connector for the transfer of sensitive personal information. I learned that Coral Andrews, the Connector's executive director, was refusing to sign the data sharing agreement required by DOH. Andrews was not willing to agree to provisions necessary to protect the privacy interests involved. I told the supervisor to stick to her guns.

A few days later, the system was scheduled to go live at midnight, the national press was watching, and at the end of the day we still did not have the signed agreement. The supervisor came in to tell me that Jim Dixon, the Connector's lawyer, had just said the Connector had agreed to our contract version, but that Andrews had signed the "wrong" version of the contract (which she wanted), and was "in a meeting" so she could not sign the correct version. Andrews wanted us to simply countersign the contract form she had signed, with the understanding that we would change it later.

This was patently absurd. I knew, Dixon knew and Andrews knew that any signed document, especially one signed by the attorney general and the DOH, would be legally binding. An oral understanding to later substitute a different contract would be worthless. It was obvious that Andrews had signed the wrong document on purpose and then made herself unavailable as a cheap and stupid little ploy. When I was a younger lawyer, such behavior would infuriate me. However, after years of dealing with similar ploys, I knew just what I had to do to fix this.

I got Dixon on the phone. I had previously known him and thought he was ethical and honest. I surmised he was being told to do this by Andrews, but it didn't matter, as we were down to the wire. I started out calmly but quickly escalated both my tone and volume, telling him loudly and with menace that in thirty years of negotiating contracts this was one of the cheapest stunts I had ever seen and that if he did not find

Andrews, get her to sign the right document and deliver it to my office within thirty minutes, I would be calling up all of the TV stations who were watching and tell them that we were pulling the plug because of Andrews's and Dixon's bad faith. I was fully prepared to follow through on my threat because they had given me no choice. That appeared to get the job done. Twenty-five minutes later, Dixon came up to my office with the proper signed agreement. Unbelievable. But the Connector went online that night as scheduled.

Special Interests

Because the stakes are high in matters that come before government, special interests such as businesses, industries and ideological advocacy groups are often involved in trying to get government to do things that benefit them. There are also many people and organizations that try to represent what they believe is the public interest. Sometimes such public interest groups are outmanned and outgunned, since they usually do not command the same level of money and support. But they can also prevail, since the arena is a public forum. In my view, special interests are not inherently evil, or bad, but merely people and entities trying to get legislation, policies and decisions adopted that are favorable to their interests. Special interests have long been a part of our democracy, as they have a right to have their points of view heard and considered. It is, however, critical that we do not allow money to simply overwhelm and drown out other viewpoints, especially those of public interest groups. Any influence peddling and money contributions should be done openly and transparently, not behind closed doors, so that the public can see what is happening.

Gov. Abercrombie used to tell me that "Special interests are okay, as long as they can be made to serve the public interest." Since the resources of government are limited, if the interests of certain groups can be made congruent and aligned with the public interest, then a win-win situation can be established. Sometimes governments enter into public private partnership (PPP) agreements, in which business interests collaborate with government to build infrastructure or provide services by putting up capital and receiving profits. It is where special interests operate to the detriment of the public interest that things become problematic. It is in the government's interest to work with special interests if they can be harnessed to accomplish aspects of the public good. It is also critical for government to prune back special interest objectives that are harmful to the larger community.

So the question always is how do we get special interests to align with the public interest? Or how do we get the public interest to be paramount and have special interests fall in line, as opposed to having the special interests subvert or subordinate the public interest? This is an age-old problem that politics and democracies have always dealt with and will continue to deal with.

Special interests are often represented by professional lobbyists in state-level politics. Most lobbyists I have met at both the state and national levels are highly professional. They are straightforward, do their jobs, provide information to support their clients' point of view and try to demonstrate how their clients' interests align with the public interest. However, that is not always the case. The following are a few stories of unusual but interesting encounters with special interests. While they are the exception to the more boring stories of lobbyists doing their jobs in a straightforward manner, they provide a cautionary tale about the darker side of politics, which public officials must guard against.

Shortly after being appointed, I received a call from a legislative leader for a meeting. No topic was mentioned. I showed up and was ushered into a large conference room where a lobbyist for Liberty Dialysis–Hawaii was waiting for me. He introduced himself and told me he was an important supporter of the governor. He then proceeded to lecture me that the Office of the Attorney General was conducting a wrongful investigation into the billing practices of his client with the Department of Health. He demanded that I immediately put a stop to the investigation. I was taken aback, especially since I had never met this guy and had not heard of this matter before. Nonetheless, I politely said I would look into it and left.

It happened that I had a meeting with Gov. Abercrombie later that day, so I mentioned what had transpired. The governor just chuckled. He said, "Don't worry about it. This kind of thing happens. Just look into it and do the right thing."

I went back and looked into the matter. I found out that the attorney general's office had an active investigation into Liberty Dialysis for fraudulent billings in violation of clear Medicaid guidelines. I talked with the deputy attorneys general doing the investigation and learned that Liberty Dialysis had improperly overbilled the State millions of dollars. This lobbyist was asking me to put a halt to a meritorious investigation and claim. It was obvious that his client was prepared to try and use creative methods to manipulate the State into letting them continue the illegal practices without consequence. Brazen, but not surprising.

Needless to say, I did not follow the direction of the lobbyist. Instead, I did the exact opposite. Because there were complicated billings involving thousands of transactions and millions of dollars, I made sure that the deputy attorneys general hired experienced outside lawyers and consultants who could assist in prosecuting the case for false claims and fraudulent billings. As I write this, an administrative hearings officer has ruled that Liberty Dialysis received overpayment from the State of $7.5 million. A false claims (qui tam) lawsuit has been brought against Liberty Dialysis, and the case is coming up for trial.

Dealing with lobbyists is a fact of public life that cannot be avoided. I always tried to listen politely but not suspend critical thinking. On a few rare occasions I encountered lobbyists who acted as if they owned you, or were lecturing a wayward child, telling me that I needed to support something or other, intimating that I was somehow beholden to them. I am sure that there are some politicians who are beholden to certain interests. Of course, I was not elected, since I was appointed, and Hawai'i's ethics rules precluded me from accepting much from anyone. Still, I remember one conversation at a Democratic Attorneys General Association (DAGA) dinner in Seattle with a national lobbyist who had consumed too much wine. She was insistent that I needed to take some action in favor of her client and was appalled that I could even consider the other side's perspective. On another occasion, the national chief lobbyist for Expedia arranged to sit next to me at a DAGA dinner after we had just filed a lawsuit to force Expedia and other online travel companies to pay millions of dollars as their fair share of taxes for selling hotel rooms in Hawai'i. Although we had a pleasant dinner, I did not discuss the case with him.

I filed that lawsuit almost immediately after taking office, after both Gov. Abercrombie and I were contacted by private attorneys who specialized in tax cases and had been unsuccessfully proposing such a lawsuit to the State for years. Gov. Linda Lingle, Gov. Abercrombie's predecessor, had apparently refused to authorize the lawsuit, even though tens of millions of dollars in taxes were at stake and the State faced fiscal shortfalls. We retained the lawyers and filed suit. Lobbyists for some of the online travel companies had a local tourism official contact me to argue that the lawsuit would harm tourism, as online travel companies would stop selling hotel rooms if they had to pay taxes. I thought that rationale was poppycock, but they were entitled to their point of view.

The lawsuit proceeded, and a few years later the Hawai'i Supreme Court ruled that online travel companies had to pay Hawai'i general excise taxes just like other hotels and rental car companies. The lawsuit resulted in judgments of more than $50 million immediately and continuing tax payments to this day.

The push and pull in the arena of different governmental officials, special interests and people simply trying to get their way can certainly be rough and tumble, but it is a fact of life in politics. Because of the importance of government policies, the impact upon peoples' lives and the large amounts of money at stake, there will always be actors seeking to bend matters in their favor. I encountered many instances of people vying for power, policies, money, solutions, advantage; some outcomes I supported, and other actions I abhorred. There were people trying to help others and others trying to get results I thought were harmful. All were using whatever tools and leverage they could to accomplish their goals. It was simply an unavoidable part of the landscape.

As you can see from my experiences, being a public official means that many people—other legislators, officials and special interests—may try to test you and do anything to get their way. Politicians who deal with lobbyists and special interests must have their moral compass and antennae up and be careful, for it is easy to lose one's way with blandishments of money and power. While most people I encountered were professional and respected norms of decorum, some of the actors were boorish or crossed a line of appropriate behavior. Although initially surprised, I quickly learned to deal with all of them. I would take a meeting with almost anyone and listen to their proposals while trying to critically assess various courses of action. Most importantly, I felt then and continue to believe that the best way to approach the actions and decisions within my sphere was on as principled a basis as possible, with fidelity to the law, the constitutions and the public good.

| 4 |

A Job Like No Other

When I accepted the job of attorney general, I thought it would be very broad, wide-ranging, with many different roles. Taking the job was a leap of faith, as I did not know what it would really be like. I underestimated how large it really was. It was not until I was on the job for several months that I truly appreciated the breadth, depth and scope of the role.

Primarily, the attorney general is a lawyer, concerned with how the law affects the State. The attorney general functions as a traditional lawyer in many instances, representing clients, opining as to the law, providing advice and counsel to the governor, the legislature and most departments and agencies as to how to legally accomplish their goals and initiatives and representing the State's interests in courts, boards and administrative forums.

But the role of the attorney general is much larger than simply being a traditional lawyer representing clients. The attorney general sits at the intersection of law, politics and government, and is a constitutional officer. In Hawai'i, the attorney general has the power to determine how to resolve most litigation and makes decisions as to legal policy matters. In addition to specific powers granted by the constitution and laws, the attorney general also has soft powers to convene, use the bully pulpit of the office and provide presence at events to shine a spotlight on issues. In my view, the most important aspects of the job of attorney general are to use the powers of the office to improve the lives of people and try to be a force for positive change. While the intellectual challenges of interesting legal issues were fascinating, working on issues where we could make a difference, such as social justice or helping the environment, were the most satisfying and meaningful to me.

Toto, We're Not in Private Practice Anymore

I soon learned that the practice of law as attorney general is very different from the practice of law that I had experienced throughout my career. The Department of the Attorney General is a large law firm like no other. It has more than twice as many lawyers as the largest private law firms in Hawai'i. The department handled every conceivable legal problem for the State, representing and advising the governor, all of the departments and agencies, the legislature and even the judiciary.

The scope of the legal problems we handled was immense. There were run-of-the-mill cases involving accidents, business contracts, land leases, child support, child protective services, collections, employment disputes, tax disputes, etc. But there were also cutting-edge cases involving constitutional principles. What restrictions can be forced on protestors seeking to exercise their First Amendment rights and disrupt an international conference? If churches use state school buildings on the weekends for worship, or the legislature opens sessions with prayer, does this violate the prohibition on establishing religion? What emergency powers can the governor invoke in the face of tsunamis or hurricanes? For sheer breadth and volume of interesting legal issues, the department was like a giant candy store. When friends would complain to me about some vexing legal problem that government needed to solve, I would tell them to take a number and get in line.

Because of the scope of the office, I had to learn a lot of new laws, starting with the powers I could wield as attorney general. The powers of the attorney general are substantial and spelled out in Hawai'i's constitution and the implementing laws. Decisions by the Hawai'i Supreme Court and the supreme courts of other states have also provided guidance. By law, the attorney general has authority and control over all litigation of the State, except where an agency has been given that specific power by the legislature. I also was in charge of establishing legal policies for the State. As attorney general, I thus was a decision maker, or as President George W. Bush would say, "a decider."

The perspective of the attorney general as a lawyer is very different from that of a private attorney. Where before I had a small number of clients as a civil trial attorney, as attorney general I had hundreds of clients, as well as the responsibility, within my sphere of influence, to think about what was best for the 1.3 to 1.4 million people in Hawai'i. My view was that I should think about what was best not just for whoever happened to be a client, but what was best for the State and the community as a whole. That's a different perspective than thinking about the narrow interests of one client and trying to assert their interests over others. That meant we should understand how the law would work for everyone, not just the ascendency of a particular interest. We also looked at how the law would be implemented to balance, harmonize and take into account the overall goals of the State as well as many other interests and considerations. This was a daunting, meaningful and substantial responsibility.

As a result, my perspective and approach to the role changed. For private lawyers, the client's interests are paramount. Private lawyers can make recommendations and provide guidance. But ultimately they must follow the client's wishes, unless illegal behavior is involved. After all, it is the client's case, not the attorney's. If the case is won or lost, the client's money is won or lost. In a criminal case, it is the client, not the attorney, who does the time if the case is lost.

Government lawyers are also keenly aware of their clients' interests, but it is a somewhat different perspective. The attorney general has no shortage of clients. While attorneys in private practice are always seeking clients and business, the attorney general is mandated by law to represent everyone and every agency in state government, with only a few exceptions. I used to tell the deputies that the great thing about being in the attorney general's office was that the clients could not fire us. Of course, the flip side was that we also could not fire the clients, no matter how difficult, obstreperous or cantankerous they might be. Moreover, the ultimate client was the State, not the particular legislator, employee or head of a department.

While we would provide advice and counsel to the governor, the legislators and department heads so they could make decisions on numerous policy and administrative matters, in almost all litigated cases before the courts, the attorney general, rather than the client, had the power to make the ultimate decisions on how the case is handled, even if that was contrary to what the agency or department sometimes wanted. On occasion, we would have to tell powerful people, "No." Sometimes individual State employees or agency heads wanted to control the litigation so that they could make a point, take an ideological position or vindicate their own personal interests. Sometimes they wanted to assert positions that were at odds with long-standing policies or positions the State had taken in other litigation. It made for interesting and sometimes heated discussions. But I had the constitution and law on my side.

One of the first things lawyers are supposed to ask themselves when they get a new matter is, "Who is the client?" Whose interest is the lawyer supposed to assert and protect? In private practice, an attorney and law firm can usually only represent one client in a matter, and cannot have divided loyalties or conflicts of interest, unless the client consents in writing to the conflict. This rule, firmly embedded in the law, is there to protect both the clients and the lawyers, so that the lawyers don't have too many masters.

But the attorney general, by statute and case law, is a special office, not subject to the same conflict of interest rules that govern private attorneys. The attorney general is mandated to represent almost everyone in state government, and that can only work if the attorney general has an exemption from normal conflict of interest rules. Of course, we would still protect the clients' individual interests by setting up different teams of attorneys from different supervisory units to represent multiple clients who might be adverse or at odds. Each team would be "walled off" (kept separate) from the other teams, so they could zealously represent their client's interests.

Because the attorney general gives advice and representation to the legislature, the governor and many others, there were times when competing actors wanted us to come up with an answer that only served their narrow interests and desires on a particular issue. In such cases, it was always extremely important that we gave correct and consistent advice to all clients as to what the Constitution and the laws mandated. Where the law was unsettled or gray, we would also tell the clients of the uncertainty and let them know the risk factors of what the courts might decide.

The attorney general also makes decisions about legal policy for the State and gives opinions to the legislature and other departments as to the constitutionality and legality of statutes, bills, actions, decisions and initiatives. The attorney general has the power to interpret laws and the constitution when there are gray areas that have not previously been decided. By statute, the attorney general is authorized to issue formal opinions. By case law, although the courts are not bound by such opinions, they are considered as highly instructive or persuasive.

The attorney general also has soft powers, powers that are not specifically set forth in the constitution or the statutes, but which are powers nonetheless and go hand in hand with the Office of the Attorney General. One of the powers of the attorney general that I learned early on is the power to convene. It is the power to shine a spotlight on a problem to convene various representatives from business, government, the community and other experts to focus on and look at a problem.

For example, I convened a working group of law enforcement officials and victim advocates to improve the handling and coordination between agencies of domestic violence cases. Domestic violence is a complex and multifaceted problem that law enforcement and various advocates and community organizations have long tried to address. We brought a working group of police chiefs, supervisors and line officers together with advocates and community organizations to foster better communication and shared projects. I believe we were successful in improving collaboration to help domestic violence victims.

Another soft power of the attorney general is simply to call people up and make suggestions. One such episode occurred when Daniel Dae Kim, one of Hawai'i's superstar actors, who was starring in the hit TV series *Hawaii Five-0*, posted a challenge on his Facebook page to encourage people in the Islands to vote. He asked his followers to send him a picture of themselves in the voting booth so that they could be entered into a drawing for a chance to visit the *Hawaii Five-0* set during filming. Voter turnout in Hawai'i is notoriously low, so this was certainly a well-meant gesture, and it got publicity. Unfortunately, the law in Hawai'i and elsewhere prohibits offering or giving people something of value to vote or not vote.

I personally reached out and called Kim's publicist to tell her the problem and suggest that they walk back the offer. Surprisingly, the publicist refused and told me that their Los Angeles lawyers had said this was fine. She was sure their lawyers knew more about the laws of Hawai'i than our office. I asked her to please have Kim call me. The next day, Kim and I spoke. I explained the law and that we did not want to make this a big deal, but that we needed him to cancel his offer. Kim had attended law school before becoming a successful actor. He quickly understood and graciously agreed to walk back his offer the next day. By making a call and having a conversation, I was able to get the necessary result.

The attorney general also has the soft power of the bully pulpit and the power of the press release. We could call up the press and the TV stations to publicize a program or policy, such as a Drug Take Back program, gathering old and unused medications, or publicizing the Internet Crimes Against Children program that went after online child predators. We usually could get coverage. Not always, and not always the front page or the six o'clock news. But more often than not, if there was a public purpose, the press would think that what we were doing was important enough to make the news cycle.

Guardians of the Process

One very important perspective for the attorney general and all government attorneys is the obligation to look out for the overall interests of the entire system of government. Don Kitaoka, a long-serving attorney at the Office of the Corporation Counsel for the City & County of Honolulu, once told me that government attorneys were the "guardians of the process." Indeed. It is critical that government processes follow the rule of law, meaning that the law is applied fairly and evenhandedly. This is a bedrock principle of American justice, which fosters trust and allows society to function in an orderly fashion. It means that everyone should be treated equally before the law, and no one is above it. When people have faith that the laws and processes are fair, they can trust and rely upon the system of government. Government attorneys have a duty of fidelity and loyalty to uphold the rule of law and guard the process of government.

In my view, all attorneys need to know who their client is and what their interests are. In addition, for the attorney general and all of the deputies, it is equally important to make sure that the process of government works for everyone, not just the client. While a private lawyer is supposed to work only for a particular outcome for his or her client, government attorneys must also consider the larger interests that the process is fair and that justice is done. As I studied the office and the powers of the attorney general, I felt that this was an important responsibility.

For example, we needed to make sure that boards, commissions and agencies all functioned in accordance with the law. One of the important duties of the deputy attorneys general was to attend meetings of boards, commissions and agencies, providing legal advice on the spot if needed. A prominent attorney friend suggested that this was a waste of the deputies' time, and that we could save a lot of money if the deputies did not attend those meetings, only responding to legal questions as needed. This suggestion was exactly backwards. Many government decisions occur through actions of lay citizen volunteers who serve on boards and commissions, who often are not knowledgeable about laws or governmental processes. The deputies are there to make sure that the citizen members follow proper procedures and have the benefit of legal advice so that their decisions are legal. Without such timely advice, procedures could be violated or decisions could be made contrary to law, which would mean they would have to be undone and redone in the future, losing valuable time and possibly giving rise to lawsuits.

On other occasions, politicians suggested that we bend the laws or provide special treatment for a political objective or their friends or acquaintances. Gov. Abercrombie and I had one meeting with a county mayor who wanted the attorney general to declare a state lease of a hotel in default, because the lessee was not maintaining the hotel property to the satisfaction of the mayor. The problem with that request was that the state lease was fully paid up and not in default at all! On another occasion, a state legislator requested that the attorney general not prosecute a staffer who had misused a government credit card, purchased personal computers and refused to pay the monies back. Special treatment for a legislator's staff? These types of requests were easy to refuse.

Some Clients Are More Equal Than Others

For any attorney general, one of the major clients, if not the most important one, is the governor. The relationship with the governor is one of the key relationships for the functioning of state government. While relationships with legislative leaders and cabinet officials are also important, because the governor is the chief executive, he or she will set a lot of the tone, agenda and pace for what happens in state government. Since the attorney general is charged with making sure that all initiatives are legal, it's critical that the attorney general knows about plans to provide timely input so initiatives and programs do not violate the law.

In states that elect the attorney general, the relationship with the governor can sometimes be rocky when the two people in the offices are political rivals. I recall my friend Gary King, the attorney general of New Mexico and a Democrat, describing his difficult relationship with Gov. Susana Martinez, a Republican, since King was planning to run for governor against her. New Mexico was involved in critical negotiations with other states over the allocation of water from the Colorado River Basin, but because the two of them were political rivals, King was having difficulty in scheduling any meetings with Gov. Martinez to discuss such negotiations.

In Hawai'i, as in four other states, the attorney general is appointed by the governor. I personally think this is a better way to go, as it generally aligns the attorney general with the intention and agenda of the governor and tends to take politics out of the equation.

However, when I first became attorney general, I did not have the kind of access to the governor that allowed a close interaction with him. Access to the governor was highly restricted, so I would have to either make an appointment or be summoned to see him. After a few months, I learned that other people were complaining about the lack of access to the governor. It appeared to me that the governor's staff initially wanted to protect him from a perceived onslaught of special interests and people with their hands out trying to get something from government. But Gov. Abercrombie was a very smart man who did not need such protection, especially from the attorney general he had appointed.

Kalbert Young, the director of finance, suggested to the governor's team that instead of restricted access, he as the head of the Department of Budget and Finance, and I as the attorney general, should meet regularly with the governor to keep tabs on what was going on and stay abreast of emerging issues. The governor and his staff agreed, and shortly thereafter the two of us were participating in regular weekly meetings with the governor and his key staff at the end of the day on Tuesdays and Thursdays. Generally around 5 p.m., we would spend an hour talking about what had happened during the day and week, what issues were arising, whether such issues posed legal or financial problems and whether either of us needed to do anything to address those issues.

This was a matter of trust. One of the big factors, obviously, in any organization is being able to work with people you trust so you can speak candidly about what you're trying to do so you can get an honest assessment of the plan and any problems that might exist. Gov. Abercrombie and his people, to my immense gratification, trusted me enough to allow me to be in the inner circle to help advise the governor. Many times, an issue would come up, and it would have no legal importance, so I would not be overly concerned about it. But other times, there would be a legal dimension on some new initiative, and I could start looking at whether there were problems and consult with deputy attorneys general about such issues.

I thus had a close-up view of decision-making and policy making at the very highest levels of government. I got to watch Gov. Abercrombie in action, see his values and thought processes, and see how cabinet directors and other very accomplished people performed in the crucible of the moment. It was exciting, exhilarating and heady, and I learned a lot.

When I first started attending these meetings, which continued on through my entire term of office, the governor said to me, "You handle the law, but leave the politics to me." I took this to mean that the governor certainly wanted my advice on legal issues, but did not want me to try to advise him on political matters. Of course, that did not mean that I was shut out from all political discussions, as many times there would be political issues that came up that I would simply be aware of, or issues that had both legal and political dimensions, such as labor disputes with the Hawaii State Teachers Association (HSTA).

Working with the governor was a true pleasure, because he was smart, forthright, spoke his mind, had a sharp and quick intellect, and was full of energy. He was always approachable, although he could be intimidating at times and was not afraid to challenge an argument or call out fools. But Gov. Abercrombie also believed in his team and generally did not try to micromanage. One of the qualities I appreciated about Gov. Abercrombie was his ability to be decisive. He was comfortable enough in his own skin and with his own intellect that he could listen to a problem even on short notice and quickly make a decision.

I also enjoyed working with the governor's staff, particularly Bruce Coppa, who had become the second chief of staff to the governor, and Blake Oshiro, the deputy chief of staff serving with Coppa. Coppa had been a political consultant in the private sector for many years and was smart, knowledgeable and well connected. Oshiro has served in the House as a representative and had risen to be the majority leader before becoming the deputy chief of staff. Both had good political instincts and were highly capable individuals.

In my view, the chief of staff and deputy chief of staff positions were extremely important positions, critical to the success of a governor's administration. I have heard others who served in the chief of staff position express that they did not want to be "the governor." But in my analysis, that is exactly what the position requires. In many ways the chief of staff is an alter ego of the governor and fills a role as gatekeeper, intermediary and even shadow governor who can help act for the governor when necessary. The chief of staff can take meetings with people when the governor needs to maintain distance and plausible deniability for political or other reasons. The chief of staff can communicate information and policies while giving the governor space to rethink choices or decisions made on the fly.

When Gov. Abercrombie came into office, he had a New Day vision that he had been working on for some time, which provided a blueprint and values for the new administration on a host of issues and policies, including the environment, fiscal responsibility, law enforcement, prison reform and many other initiatives. The governor convened regular monthly cabinet meetings to communicate information and direction to other cabinet officials. These meetings were generally informational, since the group was large, whereas the smaller meetings I had with the governor and his staff in his office were more intimate and included more of an opportunity for back and forth discussion.

Gov. Abercrombie also sought to stimulate and inspire the cabinet intellectually. He let us know that he personally read various meditations and the works of philosophers each morning to inspire himself, and in a similar vein would occasionally read the words of Dietrich Bonhoeffer and sometimes obscure nineteenth-century monks at cabinet meetings before discussions of the New Day policies and implementation. Gov. Abercrombie also arranged periodic evening salons for the cabinet, featuring conversations with thought-provoking individuals such as Joseph Stiglitz, a Nobel laureate economist. Working with the governor was enjoyable to me, as there was always something going on.

Showing Up

Another important aspect of the job was just to show up. Once I became attorney general, I had lots of invitations to do things. I was invited to events, receptions, speaking engagements, political gatherings and ceremonies. I was suddenly a lot more popular than I had been as a private attorney. Of course, it wasn't me as an individual who was being invited, it was the Officc of the Attorney General.

I felt that it was important to accept as many of these invitations as I could, and not just for the rubber chicken dinners. I believe it is important for public officials to participate in public life, to be active in the community and be accessible to people. Public officials, such as the attorney general, don't just represent themselves at events. They represent the office, the State and the participation of the office in the life of the community. It's important that public officials participate so that people at these events know they are appreciated. You can also learn an awful lot by just showing up.

Sometime in his second year of office, Gov. Abercrombie required all of the cabinet officials and deputy directors to attend monthly neighborhood board meetings, to provide regular reports of new initiatives and policies, and provide a mechanism for feedback to the community. We would give a report from the governor and answer questions. The neighborhood boards are composed of elected citizen volunteers, who take up issues of concern relating to their neighborhoods. The police and fire departments would come and deliver reports and answer questions or concerns. The city councilpersons and state legislators would come as well. The meetings occurred in the evenings, so citizens could attend. The meetings would last for several hours. I attended the Diamond Head/Kapahulu Neighborhood Board.

Initially I did not like having to go to these meetings. Sometimes the meetings were long, and sometimes the people participating were not able to communicate well or articulate their thoughts. There were also intelligent people who had ideological points of view that they wanted to expound upon at length. I had never participated in neighborhood board meetings before, and thought them unnecessary, as I believed any really important issues would eventually surface at the legislature.

But over the course of attending these meetings for a couple of years I completely changed my perspective. I grew to appreciate the wisdom of having the neighborhood board meetings and having myself and other cabinet officials attend them. It was not just to communicate the governor's message. Instead, it was a two-way street where I could both give out and get information about the concerns that people had so this could be communicated back to the governor.

It took me awhile, but I finally realized that these meetings are truly democracy in action, where people can air their concerns, debate and question what is going on in their communities and surface issues about how government is actually functioning in their daily lives. Democratic government is all about making sure that the government has the consent of the governed. These meetings were one important way to do that.

I had a similar change of heart over time about the role and importance of district courts in the judiciary. District courts are the courts in Hawai'i of lower jurisdiction—traffic violations, landlord-tenant disputes, claims worth less than $25,000, petty misdemeanors and infractions. For most of my career I have practiced in the circuit courts, which have larger dollar value cases, larger issues and unlimited monetary jurisdiction. For many years, I felt that district courts were inferior courts, not as "important" as circuit courts.

But after making a few appearances in district court, I came to realize that for the people involved, their cases were just as important to them as the cases in circuit court were to the litigants there. The money might be less, but the cases and impact meant no less to the people involved. More importantly, because the volume of cases in the district courts was many times larger than the cases in the circuit courts, most people's ideas about justice and the judiciary came in the district courts, not the circuit courts. The district courts are where "the rubber meets the road," where most people experience and decide whether the process is fair, just and evenhanded. If people are to believe in and support the rule of law, it is critical that their experience with the courts at any level be fair and positive.

All of these experiences helped me to learn and appreciate the many powers and facets of the role of attorney general and how those powers could be used to advance the overall goals of improving people's lives and making things better. I got a lot of help from the many dedicated deputy attorneys general in the office. That assistance was invaluable in tackling the larger issues that came before me. For that I remain very, very grateful.

| 5 |

Social Justice Matters

Governments must address the problems that confront their communities, and some of the most pressing problems of states and cities have roots in issues arising out of social inequality. Issues of race, gender and sexual orientation, to name a few, have been the battleground of conflict and upheaval for many years in Hawaii and throughout the nation. These issues are important because they go to the heart of how government can ensure that everyone can live, work and cooperate together for the greater good, with dignity and respect for all.

We have all been taught, since grade school, the lofty ideals of the Declaration of Independence and the Constitution, that promised that "all men are created equal" and should have equal opportunity and equal protection under the laws. I believe deeply in those ideals, and I think the majority of Americans do, too. Unfortunately, the reality of our society and communities does not always match such aspirational goals, and there are widespread inequities in wealth, socioeconomic status, power and opportunity. Many problems that governments and attorneys general must deal with, such as racial and sexual discrimination, poverty, crime and homelessness, have their roots in such inequities.

In addressing such problems, it's important for those in government to have a perspective and understanding of the historical background that got us to this point, so that laws can be enforced and enacted, and policy solutions can be fashioned, with empathy and understanding to actually solve such problems and not exacerbate them.

My personal perspective on social justice matters, and what I brought to the table as attorney general in approaching such issues, was shaped in a number of different ways, primarily through the lens of race. This included growing up as a person of color, a minority, a Chinese American in mostly white communities, learning about my heritage and identity in college, learning in law school about historical discrimination against Asian Americans, and living and working in Hawaii. My background in race and social justice issues affected the choices I made as to which issues I wanted to concentrate on when I was in office. More importantly, the legacy of governmental actions in these areas will affect how these and other new but related issues are dealt with in the future, both in Hawaiʻi and nationally.

Matters of Race

Looking back, I believe that my experiences growing up made me aware of social justice and fairness issues and gave me an understanding of how marginalized people and communities can be harmed and impaired by discrimination and disparate treatment. I grew up in predominantly white communities as my father's career took us to different places in California. There were few Chinese Americans in these communities, but I was generally accepted, had good opportunities and had good friends who were mostly white. When we would visit my grandparents in San Francisco's Chinatown, it always seemed exotic and foreign, since it was so different from the white suburban communities where we lived. However, while the communities where we lived were familiar, I was always conscious that I was different, and there was always a slight sense of being an outsider and not quite belonging.

Although I did not personally suffer any significant incidents of overt racial discrimination and ignored the occasional slights, my parents certainly experienced discrimination. In 1961, we moved to La Cañada, a conservative wealthy white Los Angeles suburb, where my father had gotten a job as the minister of Christian education for the La Cañada Presbyterian Church. No realtor would sell our family a house in the community, because we were Chinese. At that time, many houses in California had restrictive deed covenants that prohibited sales to non-whites. It was embarrassing for the church and one of the most significant examples of discrimination that we experienced as a family. Thankfully, the church solved the issue by having a church member contractor build a new house and sell it to my parents. Those discriminatory deed restrictions were only struck down in California in the late 1960s.

Not all experiences of my family as people of color were ill-intentioned. Some were just born of ignorance. My mother recently reminded me of an episode in the late 1950s when we lived in Davis, California, where a branch of the University of California was located. The Faculty Wives Club (hopefully now an anachronistic name) was throwing a going-away party and decided to have a Chinese-themed event. Some of the church women asked my mother if she would bring her opium pipe and wear her kimono. Such requests were stunning in both their ignorance and unwitting racist overtones. Chinese people did not all have opium pipes and use opium, heroin or other drugs. Kimonos were worn by Japanese, not Chinese women. Yet such statements were typical of the time, when even well-intentioned whites might try to relate to Asian Americans, but in ways that emphasized foreignness and differences.

As I grew up in the 1950s and 1960s, the myth of Chinese and Japanese Americans as model minorities was in vogue as examples of minorities who had achieved success by being quiet, industrious and hardworking, in contrast to the vocal protests, demonstrations and even riots of the civil rights movement. This myth favors Asian Americans over Blacks and Latinos but falls apart under scrutiny because it ignores vast historical differences between Asian Americans and Blacks, Latinos and Native Americans, who were subject to slavery, colonization and misappropriation of lands. The myth also obscures the struggles of other Asian and Pacific Islander communities who have not achieved economic success. Yet even with the possible advantages of this myth, Asian Americans have faced and continue to encounter discrimination in insidious forms like those experienced by my parents.

Of course, a lot of this passed me by as I was growing up. But when I attended Occidental College in the early 1970s, I began to learn about the history of Asian Americans in the United States. I met other Asian American students and learned about their efforts to get together, communicate and organize around civil rights issues, inspired by the civil rights movement. My older brother, Stephen, was active in the Asian American movement and traveled around the country meeting and working with other Asian American students and organizations. I attended some conferences for Asian American students and was active with the Asian American Student Association at Occidental. One of my advisors was Dr. Franklin Odo, who helped to create Asian American Studies and other ethnic studies programs, and became a prominent Asian American scholar and historian. It was a revelation to me to learn about Asian American history, as that is a subject not usually taught in most schools. Even colleges and universities only began teaching such subjects in the 1970s and '80s as a result of students of color demanding ethnic studies programs.

I had never consciously put a name on or thought about my experience as a person of color growing up in white communities, since it was just what I experienced. But this contact with the Asian American movement made me much more conscious of my identity as a Chinese American, the whole issue of being a person of color, and my understanding of the civil rights movement and the quest for social justice.

I became increasingly interested in learning about my heritage and identity and began studying more about Asia. In my junior year at Occidental, I received an international fellowship to undertake independent study and research for nine months in Hong Kong. There I became friends with some Chinese American students who fortuitously had arranged a two-month trip to the People's Republic of China and invited me along. We were in the first wave of Americans allowed into China following President Richard Nixon's "ping-pong diplomacy" initiative in 1972. Seeing the country of my ancestry, being in a nation of people who looked like me and seeing the accomplishments and energy of the Chinese people was a fantastic and affirming experience and made me proud of my heritage.

When I went to law school in Berkeley, I became friends with other Asian American law students and lawyers and learned much more about the history of Asian Americans. I became a teaching assistant for Asians and the Law, an undergraduate course about legal decisions involving Asian Americans. One of the most important cases we studied was *Korematsu v. United States*, in which the Supreme Court upheld the conviction of Fred Korematsu for refusing to comply with Executive Order 9066, a US presidential order resulting in the forced incarceration of 120,000 loyal Japanese American citizens during World War II. This case had been infamous for many decades, as the incarceration destroyed many Japanese American communities and a great deal of their wealth, based only upon flimsy racist claims by some military leaders that Japanese Americans were spies and saboteurs.

The course was taught by Dale Minami, a lawyer who had recently graduated from Berkeley and was active in Asian American civil rights issues. Minami and a team of my other law school friends, including Don Tamaki, Eric Yamamoto, Edward Chen, Lori Bannai and Leigh-Ann Miyasato, brought a lawsuit against the United States government several years later that overturned the conviction of Korematsu using materials and papers uncovered by historian Peter Irons. Those documents showed that Order 9066 was based on false racist hysteria, that US military commanders concealed the true facts that Japanese Americans were not a military threat and that J. Edgar Hoover of the Federal Bureau of Investigation had determined that there was no espionage threat. Shockingly, even the United States solicitor general chose not to inform the Supreme Court of these facts and that the claim of national security to support the internment was based upon lies and falsehoods. In 2011, Neal Katyal, the acting solicitor general of the United States, issued an official confession of error, admitting that the solicitor general's office was wrong in defending the country's wartime internment policy based upon lies.

My friendships and contact with Asian American lawyers over the years kept me aware of civil rights issues and achievements in the Asian American legal community. Indeed, a number of these close friends went on to achieve notable milestones. Minami continued as a prominent civil rights lawyer and was recently honored with the 2019 American Bar Association (ABA) Medal for his work leading the *Korematsu* legal team. Edwin M. Lee, with whom I shared a house in law school, became the first Chinese American mayor of San Francisco, serving from 2011 to 2017. Chen, another housemate, became a United States district court judge. Hoyt Zia, the founding president of the National Asian Pacific American Bar Association (NAPABA), served as chief counsel for Export Administration at the US Department of Commerce during the Clinton administration. Yamamoto became a noted professor at the William S. Richardson School of Law at the University of Hawai'i, publishing many social justice books and articles, including a recent book on the *Korematsu* case. I thought about emulating their achievements and public service when the opportunity came along to become attorney general.

Diversity in Hawai'i

In reflecting on my experience as attorney general, another important factor in how I got here and what I did arose from living in Hawai'i, which is relatively unique in the United States as a multicultural, multiracial state and community. I have benefited from being in Hawai'i in immeasurable ways, not the least of which is that I have been able to succeed without experiencing disadvantage or discrimination related to issues of race. Hawai'i has long had a climate of racial tolerance along with a prevalent custom of friendly teasing about race in a gentle, nonthreatening way. This is not to say that issues of race do not exist here. Race always matters—I just believe that race matters differently in Hawai'i than the way race matters in other states on the mainland.

Hawai'i is probably the most diverse state in the Union, and Asian Americans have achieved substantial success here. Because Hawai'i has been a welcoming place with a welcoming culture, along with a history of bringing foreign Asian laborers (Chinese, Japanese and Filipinos) to work on the sugar and pineapple plantations, Hawai'i has developed an amazingly diverse population.

This cultural context, which I learned after moving to Hawai'i, helps to explain the different perceptions of race between myself and Asian American friends who had grown up in Hawai'i. At Occidental I had met and became friends with a number of Asian American students from Hawai'i. Perplexingly to me, many of them did not seem to share my growing perceptions that Asian Americans were minorities who had historically experienced discrimination and should be concerned with social justice issues. My Asian American law student friends from Hawai'i were much more conscious of social justice issues. But moving to Hawai'i after law school showed me the differing experiences of Asian Americans in Hawai'i from Asian Americans on the mainland.

Hawai'i is a unique multicultural environment. Asians, not whites, are the majority population. In fact, some sources note that Hawai'i is the only state with a majority Asian American population. There is a lot of intermarriage and mixing, and many people identify with multiple ethnicities. In 2020, the US Census Bureau released statistics for Hawai'i's population that noted for people who identified as only one race, Asians (Filipino, Japanese, Chinese, Korean and other Asian) comprised 37.6%, whites comprised 25.5%, Native Hawaiian and other Pacific Islanders comprised 10.1%, with 24.2% of the population identifying as two or more races. When people identified as more than one race (which leads to totals of more than 100%), Asians comprised 57.3%, whites comprised 43.5%, Native Hawaiian and other Pacific Islanders comprised 27%, Black or African Americans comprised 3.6% and Hispanics comprised 10.7%. Importantly, in the last forty years, Asian Americans have been in the governmental halls of power as governors, legislative leaders and judges, while also rising to prominence in the local business community.

But this has not always been the case. The historical background of economics, politics and government in Hawaiʻi is very important to understand Hawaiʻi's current situation. For many years Hawaiʻi was controlled by white business interests, even though there were significant minority communities. It was not until a political revolution occurred in the 1950s and the 1960s in Hawaiʻi through the ballot box and organized labor that non-whites gained political representation. John A. Burns, who had worked to keep the Japanese Americans in Hawaiʻi from being incarcerated in World War II, put together a Democratic political coalition to challenge the Republicans for control of the state. Japanese American soldiers such as Daniel K. Inouye came back from the war and were not satisfied to be second-class citizens in their own communities and sought political power. Hawaiʻi was also undergoing labor strife, as the International Longshore and Warehouse Union (ILWU) was seeking to get decent wages and a piece of the pie that was controlled by the major corporations.

While the Democratic revolution did not happen overnight, it did happen, and the power of the ballot box allowed Asian American immigrant communities, who had created families, raised children and built houses, to go from being merely contract labor to becoming an integral part of the economic and power structure of the community. That Democratic revolution still reverberates and echoes in Hawaiʻi's politics today.

Hawaiʻi's success in fostering diversity throughout the community might serve as a model for how communities can deal with racial, ethnic and cultural differences. All of the racial groups in Hawaiʻi have generally been very accepting of other races and cultures, which has led to a lot of interpersonal relationships and intermarriage. Perhaps Hawaiʻi's experience is due to being in a smaller geographic area or being on islands; perhaps this has been a function of the welcoming Native Hawaiian culture; perhaps there are other factors at work. Perhaps Hawaiʻi is a bubble, an anomaly, that is not likely to be repeated on the mainland. Yet I remain hopeful that the experience of Hawaiʻi can, in small and large ways, provide an example for our nation of successful diversity and complementary cultures that contribute to a better overall community.

Now this is not to suggest that life in Hawaiʻi is all a bowl of cherries. There are differences. There is discrimination. There have always been people calling out the differences between the races. But the discrimination experienced in Hawaiʻi over the last several decades has generally not been against either whites or Asian Americans. Both groups constitute substantial portions of the overall population and tend to be considered majorities. Nonetheless, Native Hawaiians and other Pacific Islander groups have not fared as well, are disproportionately poorer and in important ways have been left behind. There are very few Blacks in Hawai'i, and they have reported encountering discrimination. Recent immigrant groups such as Micronesians also face more issues of discrimination, poverty and homelessness than other Asian American groups.

However, let me address a persistent urban myth that I've heard over the years—that whites face systemic discrimination in Hawai'i. Recently a friend on the mainland asked about this. That has not been my experience or observation at all. While I'm aware of some incidents involving whites and I have listened to a few new transplants to Hawai'i casually complain about "driving while white" and being stopped by local Asian American cops, I think such instances are more likely due to people from the mainland acting (and driving) more aggressively than is normally seen here, which stands out and elicits a predictable reaction. Even when such instances occur, they do not in any way rival the frequent reports in the media of traffic stops, harassment, killings and overt racist behavior against Blacks, Latinos and Asian Americans on the mainland. Although there may be racial differences in Hawai'i, in my view there are a lot less racial differences and discrimination here than in the rest of the United States.

To me, Hawai'i's diversity and accepting attitudes about race and culture have been important factors that have helped me to succeed, and they have led to good outcomes for Hawai'i. A climate of inclusion and understanding leads to people working together for mutual success and shared goals, despite differences in race or culture, and is far more positive for a community than an environment of divisiveness and discrimination. In other words, diversity has helped to define, rather than divide, Hawai'i.

Practicing Law in Hawai'i

Being a lawyer in Hawai'i, with its many races and ethnicities, also influenced and shaped my perspective on social justice issues while allowing me the opportunity to develop the skills, tools and perspective needed to serve as attorney general. Part of my perspective on social justice issues is based on simply living and experiencing how diversity in Hawai'i has allowed many people of different races to succeed and flourish. When

I moved to Hawai'i, I found its ethnic mix and large Asian American population to be very welcoming. The feeling of belonging and being a full part of the community is an intangible plus for Asian Americans in Hawai'i. I have also had many friends and relatives from the mainland tell me that they always feel very comfortable in Hawai'i because there are so many Asians here.

One of the major differentiating factors used by people in Hawai'i is not specifically race, since Hawai'i has so many people of different races, but whether a person is "local." Although being "local" could sometimes be a marker for race, the more important and overriding question has been whether a person has local roots and understanding of local culture. One common question that comes up when people in Hawai'i meet for the first time is, "Where you wen' grad?"—in which someone is asking where you graduated from high school, not college. High school was often a determinant of neighborhood, income level and a family's professional status, and knowing how to answer this question suggests that you are local.

Being Chinese American, I looked like a local, because of the many Asian Americans here. Until I opened my mouth, people would usually think that I was likely born and raised in Hawai'i. As shown by the question above, an important part of being local was the ability to speak pidgin, a local Hawai'i Creole-type amalgamation of many different languages, including Portuguese, Hawaiian, American English and Cantonese. Although many locally born Caucasians could speak pidgin, I could not, and my clumsy attempts would be met by gales of laughter from my friends.

When I was a young lawyer, I tried a case on Maui. After I won the trial and got a defense verdict, I asked to talk to the jury about the case to get feedback from them on how I did as a lawyer. When I met with some of the jurors, I was surprised that they did not want to talk about the case at all—my performance, my cross-examinations or my closing argument. Instead, they said they had a burning question for me. They said six of the jurors thought I was from the mainland, but six of the jurors thought I was local—but that I had gone to Punahou School (a somewhat exclusive private school and President Barack Obama's alma mater) and that was why I "talked funny."

Notwithstanding my lack of local roots, I have been blessed with being able to practice in Hawai'i simply as a lawyer, without being pigeonholed as an Asian American lawyer, which might have occurred had I practiced on the mainland. Because of the many Asian American lawyers in Hawai'i, I never felt that my ethnicity was a distinguishing characteristic that affected my development as a lawyer. I have always felt that my abilities and talents (such as they are) have been evaluated in Hawai'i primarily on my own merits, and not because I was an Asian American. In other words, I did not feel I had to overcome any negative baggage of being a minority lawyer or being perceived as less of a lawyer because I was a minority. I have had friends tell me they faced such challenges on the mainland, where some white lawyers regarded some minority lawyers of color as "affirmative action lawyers" who were less competent. Of course, that was and is another misconception born of ignorance and racism.

In hindsight, even beyond the ability to practice law in Hawai'i, I was the beneficiary of a timely confluence of national trends at law schools and law firms that greatly increased diversity in the field of law as I began my career. Indeed, my career as a lawyer coincided with the gradual integration of the world of law at a national level and the proliferation over time of more and more Black, Latino, Asian American and Native American lawyers. In the 1950s, the field of law was predominantly white. Lawyers for the business community, even in Hawai'i, were predominantly white.

In 1977, when I got out of law school, the picture for lawyers of color was beginning to change, but slowly. On the mainland, more lawyers of color were being brought into the large mainstream law firms as associates. But there were few minority partners in the large firms, and the path was not particularly clear that there would be. There were few role models to follow, so many lawyers of color had to forge their own paths. Over the course of my career, the number of Asian American attorneys has grown dramatically, from around 10,000 in 1990 to more than 55,000 at present. Still, there are relatively few Asian American partners in major national law firms, despite the large numbers of Asian American associates in such firms. Becoming a partner in such firms is still a very difficult road. Fortunately, a number of Asian Americans have persevered and succeeded in becoming partners, as they help to integrate the profession and serve as role models and trailblazers for young lawyers and generations to come.

The story in Hawai'i was very similar for many years. In the 1950s, the big law firms in Honolulu did not normally hire Japanese American or Chinese American lawyers, despite the large population of Asian Americans in the community and their graduation from some of the very best law schools. It was not until the 1960s and '70s that Asian American lawyers, primarily Japanese Americans, started to participate in the large mainstream law firms in Hawai'i.

By the time I joined Case & Lynch in 1977, many of those barriers for Asian American lawyers in Hawai'i had come down. Asian Americans were thoroughly involved in all aspects of state government, including the judiciary. While the major law firms in Hawai'i were still mainly white, there were a significant number of prominent Asian American lawyers who were succeeding and commanding significant business and power. This was also true for the business community, as Asian Americans achieved higher and higher levels of success in the mostly white major business organizations in Hawai'i. This trend has continued throughout my career and continues today.

My Perspective on Social Justice Issues as Attorney General

My personal experiences growing up as a person of color in white communities, along with my education as to the history of Asian Americans in America, sensitized me to issues of social justice. My experience living and working in Hawai'i showed me the substantial benefits that diversity brings to the richness and success of a community. All of these experiences led me to want the Office of the Attorney General to be on the right side of history as such issues regarding equality and dignity arose. I thought it was my duty and responsibility to be aware of the arc of history on social justice matters, and to positively impact any such issues that might arise. While I was attorney general, marriage equality for same-sex couples and various Native Hawaiian issues came to the forefront. Both areas raise questions of equality, justice, righting historical wrongs and the idea of opportunity based upon merit, not on immutable characteristics such as the color of a person's skin or sexual orientation. Those ideals come straight out of the constitutions of the United States and Hawai'i and are guiding principles for the attorney general.

After I became attorney general in 2011, I looked and found that although there had been a number of Japanese American and Korean American attorneys general in Hawai'i, I was the first Chinese American attorney general in the history of the United States. Until then, there were no Asian American attorneys general in any of the other states, but that changed quickly. Kamala Harris, who is part African American and part South Asian, became the attorney general of California in 2011. In 2015,

Douglas Chin succeeded me in Hawai'i as the second appointed Chinese American attorney general. Then in 2019 in Connecticut, William Tong became the first *elected* Chinese American attorney general in the United States. I certainly hope that there are many more.

Given the many factors that go into a successful career as an elected politician, including race and demographics, it is obviously more difficult, but not impossible, for an Asian American to win a statewide race outside of Hawai'i. While there have been a number of prominent and successful elected Asian American national politicians from other states, such as Norman Mineta and Gary Locke, most have been from Hawai'i, such as US senators Daniel K. Inouye and Mazie K. Hirono. However, this picture has been changing recently, as more Asian Americans have successfully run for office in various states.

Being Chinese American and being aware of social justice issues were important factors in how I approached certain matters and problems where social justice aspects were involved. But there were many other issues that arose, especially on a day-to-day basis, where this perspective was not a primary factor in how I approached the job. To me, the most important factors on almost all issues were the ideals and principles of the constitutions of the United States and Hawai'i and the lodestar of wanting to do what was right for the most people in Hawai'i. Even when social justice issues were involved, my oath required fealty to those principles and precedents of the law.

All in all, the job of attorney general in Hawai'i, as in other states, is about governing. It is about doing what is best for the people of Hawai'i, doing the greatest good for the greatest number. It is about moving society forward, solving problems and hoping to leave things better than the way I found them. Sometimes the issues on the table had nothing to do with race or social justice. At other times, social justice and racial or gender equity factors were central to the calculus of governing and had to be recognized and taken into account, as they reflected where we have been and impact where we are going.

Sonia Sotomayor, an associate justice of the United States Supreme Court, got a lot of grief at her confirmation hearing for having once said, "I would hope that a wise Latina woman with the richness of her experiences would more often than not reach a better conclusion than a white male who hasn't lived that life." While those who sought to tear her down claimed that she was making race out to be an overriding factor, she clarified her remark to say that anyone would have an equal opportunity to be a wise judge, regardless of their background or life experience. Thankfully, she was confirmed by the Senate to sit on the Supreme Court. The kernel of truth that I took from her remarks was that having a diverse background could provide a richer and more well-rounded approach to decision-making, so that her decisions would be better for having considered many viewpoints and not be confined to the narrow paths of the past.

There is much going on in the world today around race and how it affects people's lives and their communities. The events of 2020 and 2021, including the numerous deaths of Black men such as George Floyd, the ensuing protests involving the Black Lives Matter movement, the sharp and horrific rise of thousands of anti-Asian violence attacks, and the scapegoating of Asian Americans in the shadow of the COVID-19 pandemic, have focused attention on race in America as never before. Information about the systemic racism that has harmed Black communities over many years has become more widespread in the national media, providing education about the pervasive roadblocks faced by Blacks. Many Asian American voices and organizations, such as Helen Zia and Stop AAPI Hate, have stepped up to denounce the recent incidents of anti-Asian hatred and discrimination and show that Asian Americans will fight for their rights. Unlike prior years, 2021 seems different, like an inflection point, where our nation may become more able to positively deal with the crippling legacies of racism, implicit bias and wealth disparities because of the overwhelming support this year from many whites, other communities of color, the media and large corporate businesses. Only time will tell whether our nation can begin to heal these wounds, deal with the scars of systemic injustice and move forward.

| 6 |

No Longer Invisible

There are moments in our lives, in the lives of nations and states, when history is made and things change for the better. Hawai'i had one of those moments in 2013. In those moments, standing up and advocating for equal rights is one of the most important things an attorney general can do. It is a matter of simple social justice. The rights of gay and lesbian members of our community to be like everyone else, including the right to marry the person they love and have that marriage recognized and sanctified by the government, have been among the defining civil rights issues confronting the nation for several decades. Given my background and interest in civil rights and social justice issues, it was a great privilege to participate in a number of events that led to legalization of same-sex marriage in Hawai'i. This was one of the most personally satisfying contributions I was able to make as attorney general.

Today a large majority of Americans and people in Hawai'i agree that all people should have the right to be married and to live with the person they love, regardless of sexual orientation. However, the fight for marriage equality for gay and lesbian couples in Hawai'i and in the entire United States was anything but easy, and was long and hard fought. Indeed, that fight has been just one facet of the long, historical fight for LGBTQ (lesbian, gay, bisexual, transgender and queer) people to be free from discrimination in many areas of life. There have been cultural, legal and political fights that were noisy and acrimonious, with both ugly and beautiful moments. These fights for the hearts and minds of people on these issues continue today throughout the nation in various places, althought they generally seem to be relatively quiet now in Hawai'i.

The fight in Hawai'i over the legalization of same-sex marriage played out against the backdrop of legal battles across the nation in both state and federal courts, and in legislatures. These fights reached a watershed moment in 2013 at the United States Supreme Court in the cases of *United States v. Windsor* and *Hollingsworth v. Perry*. The decisions in those cases sparked the actions of Gov. Abercrombie and the legislature to take up the issue, change the law and make same-sex marriages legal in Hawai'i. The following is a short recap of the history that got us to the inflection point of change. Some of this I knew about because it happened in the news. Other parts I had to research and study as we handled various legal matters about these issues. I hope it's not too much legalese, but it provides context for what was to come.

Great rights in cultural issues are often decided by the courts in ruling on mundane but complex technical issues. In the *Windsor* case, Edith Windsor sought a federal tax exemption as a surviving spouse when she inherited the estate of her deceased spouse. The same-sex couple had been married under New York law, which recognized such marriages. The federal Defense of Marriage Act (DOMA) barred federal recognition of same-sex marriage, so Windsor was denied this exemption. In June 2013, the US Supreme Court, in a 5–4 decision authored by Justice Anthony Kennedy, held in *Windsor* that DOMA violated the United States Constitution Due Process Clause. In the *Hollingsworth* case, decided on the same day as *Windsor*, although not directly addressing the constitutionality of same-sex marriage, the Supreme Court declined to overturn a series of lower federal court decisions that had struck down laws banning same-sex marriages as violations of the Equal Protection Clause. The Supreme Court held that the persons challenging the *Hollingsworth* case holdings did not have standing to bring such lawsuits. The practical effect of these two rulings was to allow the legalization of same-sex marriage.

For many decades, the fight for social justice for gay and lesbian couples had been ongoing. Gay and lesbian couples have long sought equal marriage rights and recognition that discrimination on the basis of sexual orientation should be prohibited. At the same time, some religious and socially conservative groups have actively fostered and promoted the ideas that discrimination by individuals and groups against gays and lesbians is a God-given right that the government should not infringe. Some fundamentalist religious groups have argued that their heterosexual marriages would somehow be harmed by allowing same-sex couples the identical right.

Hawai'i's supreme court was in the forefront of the fight for marriage equality. In 1993, in *Baehr v. Lewin*, the Hawai'i Supreme Court became the first state supreme court to issue a ruling regarding the legality of same-sex marriage. In an opinion authored by Justice Steven Levinson, the court held that under Hawai'i's Equal Protection Clause, denying marriage licenses to same-sex couples constituted discrimination based on sex that could only be justified if the state could show a "compelling interest" to justify such discrimination. The Court drew an analogy to *Loving v. Virginia*, a United States Supreme Court case that struck down bans against interracial marriages.

The Hawai'i Supreme Court, however, was ahead of its time with its reasoning and analysis. This decision provoked a severe negative backlash across the nation and in Hawai'i as many state legislatures, fearful that their state courts might rule the same way as Hawai'i, rushed to enact constitutional amendments that stated that marriage could only be defined as a relationship between one man and one woman, thereby excluding gay couples. As a matter of legal analysis, any clause of a constitution is always considered a higher authority compared to mere statutes, so passing laws prohibiting same-sex marriage would not be enough. However, a constitutional amendment prohibiting same-sex marriage would be on an equal footing with the Equal Protection Clause, and the prohibition could stand. Numerous state legislatures across the country approved constitutional amendments with that goal in mind.

To overturn the *Baehr* decision, in 1997 a constitutional amendment defining marriage as being only between a man and a woman was proposed in Hawai'i as well. However, the progressive legislators who supported gay rights came up with a subtle strategy that would allow them to fight another day. This simple strategy became legally important fifteen years later. The procedure in Hawai'i for enacting constitutional amendments is a rigorous one by design. The framers did not want the Constitution to be amended lightly or easily. The procedure first requires approval by the legislature and then approval by the electorate. Sometimes it can take years to amend the Constitution.

If a constitutional amendment was adopted that said marriage is between a man and a woman only, and not same-sex couples, then it would enshrine the discrimination. More importantly, if times changed and became more accepting of gays and lesbians, then it would require another constitutional amendment to change and reverse the discrimination. So the progressive legislators in favor of marriage equality came up with a subtle twist and convinced their colleagues to enact a constitutional amendment which said only that the legislature would have the power to define whether marriage could only be between a heterosexual couple. This critical distinction in wording meant that the power to change the statute resided in the legislature, which could also change its mind in the future without having to undergo the full and rigorous procedure for enacting a constitutional amendment.

In 1998 the constitutional amendment passed by a large margin of almost 70%, showing that Hawai'i was still quite socially conservative and not ready to allow same-sex marriage. The legislature subsequently passed a law defining marriage as between a man and a woman. The Hawai'i courts recognized that the *Baehr* decision would have to bow to the constitutional amendment and the political will of the electorate, and held that the Hawai'i statute declaring that marriage was only between a man and a woman was valid.

In the twenty years following the *Baehr* decision, there was a gradual shift in national public opinion, as well as in Hawai'i, about acceptance of gay and lesbian relationships. More gay and lesbian people came out and let their neighbors and friends know of their sexual orientation, while at the same time underscoring that they were normal human beings. More and more, heterosexual people began to understand that gay and lesbian co-workers, acquaintances and friends were not deviants or strange aliens. Even before the *Baehr* decision, the advent of the AIDS crisis in the 1980s, which mostly affected gay communities, also put a human face on the issue of sexual orientation as heterosexual people saw that those who were dying included people like themselves, friends and colleagues. Television shows and movies that had gay leading characters became more prevalent. Gays and lesbians were shown in the media as ordinary neighbors and members of the community. Gay Pride parades and participation in community life became more commonplace.

Gay and lesbian communities were also exerting increasing economic and political power. Openly gay political candidates were getting elected, even in conservative communities. Court challenges to discriminatory laws against gay and lesbian couples continued and were brought in federal as well as state courts. Gay couples were allowed to adopt children and proved that they could be good parents. While some states had prohibited gay marriage, other states had allowed such marriages. States that had allowed gay marriage had shown that such marriages did not mean the end of the world.

In pre-modern times, Hawai'i had a long history of acceptance of gay men. The word *mahu* in the Hawaiian language referred to men who had sexual relations with other men. The accounts of European ship captains such as Captain James Cook noted the existence and role of mahu in Native Hawaiian society. Mahu were not just accepted in Native Hawaiian culture, they were also given places of power and respect as teachers of hula and keepers of cultural traditions. However, the arrival of religious missionaries in Hawai'i and the rise of European and American cultures resulted in Hawai'i becoming much like the rest of the nation in denigrating mahu, gays and lesbians.

In the 1980s, 1990s and 2000s, Hawai'i seemed to be accepting of gay and lesbians generally, in that there was no climate of open hostility or persecution. However, gays and lesbians were still not accorded full rights as citizens in a number of areas. While some legislation to address these deficiencies was pushed forward, the gay and lesbian communities in Hawai'i, perhaps in reaction to the backlash from the *Baehr* decision, were not particularly aggressive in protesting such injustices publicly or bringing court challenges to discriminatory practices.

In 1997, at the same time the constitutional amendment prohibiting same-sex marriage was passed, Hawai'i's legislature passed a "reciprocal beneficiary" law, which provided same-sex couples with some of the rights and benefits that come with marriage but was noticeably weaker than marriage. In 2009, state representative Blake Oshiro introduced a bill that would provide greater recognition of the validity of same-sex relationships by creating "civil unions" as an alternative to marriage. This law would accord same-sex couples many of the benefits of marriage without calling it marriage. It was half a loaf, but better than no loaf at all. The law was passed in the House but tabled in the Senate. In 2010, the civil unions bill was passed by the Senate but was vetoed by then-governor Linda Lingle. In 2011, a substantively similar bill allowing civil unions was again passed by the legislature, but this time it was signed into law by Gov. Abercrombie.

My participation as attorney general with these issues began at the end of 2011, when a new federal lawsuit was filed in *Jackson v. Abercrombie*, directly challenging Hawai'i's law that prohibited same-sex marriage, on the basis of the Equal Protection Clause and the Due Process Clause. The new lawsuit named as defendants both Gov. Abercrombie and Loretta Fuddy, the director of the Department of Health.

The first question we had to determine was what was the position of the attorney general in dealing with this lawsuit? Should we defend a discriminatory law because it was existing law and followed the will of the Hawai'i electorate of fourteen years before? Or should we take the position that the law was unconstitutional and discriminatory? Should we do what I thought was the right thing to do, regardless of the fact that I had taken an oath to uphold and defend the Constitution and laws of the state of Hawai'i and the United States?

I personally believed that the *Baehr* decision had been correct, if not politically palatable in its time. I also believed that gay and lesbian couples had a fundamental right to marry the person of their choice, regardless of sexual orientation or gender. Of course, my beliefs and predilections were not necessarily the decisive factor. So how to resolve the competing viewpoints and interests?

There were two precedential decisions of respected attorneys general on this issue. In 2009, California attorney general Jerry Brown, with the support of Gov. Arnold Schwarzenegger, refused to defend a court challenge against Proposition 8, a California initiative seeking a constitutional amendment prohibiting same-sex marriage. Instead, Brown told a federal court that Proposition 8 was unconstitutional. Brown's decision not to defend Proposition 8 was reinforced in 2011 by California attorney general Kamala Harris, who also refused to defend the law.

In 2011, United States attorney general Eric Holder, with the support of President Barack Obama, chose not to defend the federal DOMA law, which was being challenged in federal courts on equal protection and due process grounds by Edith Windsor. Attorney General Holder was exercising the discretion of his office not to defend a position that he believed was unconstitutional and wrong.

Gov. Abercrombie was clearly a progressive liberal Democrat who believed in striking down discrimination and upholding civil rights. There was precedent. Should we do the same?

This is where politics reared its ugly head. The issue of same-sex marriage has always been highly contentious, with many proponents and opponents, not just in the community, but in the legislature as well. The legislators in Hawai'i had debated these issues and taken opposing positions on numerous occasions as they considered civil union bills. Legislators always expect the attorney general to defend laws that the legislature has passed. If we chose not to defend the law in the *Jackson* lawsuit, then that would surely anger certain key members of the legislature.

The *Jackson* lawsuit was filed just before the 2012 legislative session started. In that session, Gov. Abercrombie was pushing some important initiatives and needed legislative support. I had my own important legislative initiative to shepherd through the legislature that year. Charleen Aina (one of the key deputy attorneys general who helped on Native Hawaiian matters) and I had recently concluded negotiations to finalize an approximately $200 million settlement with the Office of Hawaiian Affairs (OHA) over disputes that had lasted thirty years, and we needed to get legislative approval.

A number of legislators, including those in leadership, were interested in the *Jackson* lawsuit and let me know that they believed that the attorney general should defend all laws passed by the legislature regardless of their merits. Moreover, some of the legislators intimated that if we did not defend the law, this could threaten the governor's legislative agenda as well as threaten approval of any OHA deal. The legislature had previously considered and rejected prior proposals to resolve the OHA claims. We knew it might be hard to get the OHA settlement approved under the best of circumstances, but refusing to defend the law prohibiting same-sex marriage might make approval impossible. These were credible threats.

Ultimately, I believe that the attorney general has to do what he or she thinks is the right thing to do under the law and the Constitution, regardless of the political interests or pressures involved. The attorney general serves the entire state, including the governor, the cabinet, the legislators, all government employees and even the judiciary. Sometimes those interests compete and collide, and the attorney general has to determine what is required by law and the Constitution. Yet politics is often regarded as "the art of the possible," so political consequences should always be considered, if not necessarily followed, as part of the decision-making process.

My solution to this dilemma came from the unique power of the attorney general to represent multiple clients with competing positions at the same time. Unlike private attorneys, the attorney general is not limited to representing only one client in a lawsuit, even if two or more clients have competing interests. Because the *Jackson* lawsuit plaintiffs had sued both Gov. Abercrombie and the director of health, although both were official representatives of the State, we could treat them as separate clients with different positions.

We came up with the strategy to have two teams of deputy attorneys general to separately represent each of the named defendants and take two different positions. Gov. Abercrombie's team would take the position that the Hawai'i law prohibiting same-sex marriage violated the Equal Protection Clause and the Due Process Clause of the United States Constitution. Director Fuddy's team would defend the existing law as presumptively constitutional and assert the right of the legislature to make laws without interference from the courts, to say no to same-sex marriage.

But conceiving of a strategy is not always the same as putting it into action. First, I needed to convince the governor that this was the proper strategy. I met with the governor in his large, spacious office, with two-story-high ceilings and lovely koa wood paneling, filled with wonderful artwork and the portraits of previous governors. The governor was sitting behind an old historic koa desk that had been made in the 1880s. It was a fitting environment for making big decisions on the future of the people and state of Hawai'i.

Gov. Abercrombie and I talked about the *Jackson* lawsuit, the concerns raised by legislators and their leadership, and my procedural solution to such concerns. Gov. Abercrombie wanted to take a very strong, principled stance, just as President Obama and Gov. Schwarzenegger were doing, to say that, "Same-sex marriage is right. Prohibitions on same-sex marriage are wrong. The State of Hawai'i will not support a law that is unconstitutional and violates equal protection." While I agreed with the governor, I also wanted to accomplish our other goals at the legislature. After discussion, the governor agreed with my strategy.

I next met with the legislators who had voiced concerns and let them know that their voices and positions defending the law would be represented through a team of lawyers representing director Fuddy. They were fine with the strategy since it respected their position and authority. The lawsuit then went forward with the separate teams of deputy attorneys general representing opposing viewpoints. Some media commentators expressed surprise and criticized the dual positions, suggesting that the governor could not make up his mind.

Unfortunately, this criticism appeared to cause Gov. Abercrombie to reconsider his earlier approval of the strategy. I was called up to the governor's office to discuss this. I brought along Jill Nagamine, one of the deputy attorneys general who was principally working on these matters, and several other deputies. I started to explain our strategy to the governor, but he angrily interrupted me to say that my proposed plan was all wrong. The governor, who can get very impassioned, kept raising his voice louder and louder, letting me know that the strategy I had convinced him to adopt was dumb and should be abandoned. When he paused, I explained that although I personally supported his position, our plan was the best way forward.

The governor interrupted me again, emphatically arguing that this was a matter of equal protection and civil rights, and the State had to stand on the right side of history. Kate Stanley, one of the governor's political advisors, perhaps alarmed at the heated discussion, leaned over to whisper that the governor did not mean any of this personally. We went back and forth like this for about ten to fifteen minutes. The governor argued loudly and passionately that I should change the strategy and not defend the law, while I kept meeting his objections and concerns with practical reasons why my plan was better, noting that he could publicly state that as governor he fully supported marriage equality. Finally, Gov. Abercrombie almost snarled at me and said, "All right, we'll do it your way, but you'd better be right." I told him not to worry, that it would be fine.

As we left the building, Nagamine remarked, "Geez, I thought we were going to be fired on the spot, because the governor was so upset." I told them I had seen this movie before, that the governor did not mean any of his criticism personally, and that what they had seen was an occasional part of his thinking and decision-making process. Gov. Abercrombie was a passionate, caring man who at times would allow his emotions to be part of his thinking process. However worked up he might get, it was never personal, it was always about the ideas. I had not seen him get quite this worked up before, but this was a big, important issue.

The *Jackson* case proceeded with our strategy to assert two positions. The federal court initially upheld the validity of the statute, but that ruling was appealed and later vacated in light of the Supreme Court's decisions allowing same-sex marriages.

Following *Windsor* and *Hollingsworth*, there was a groundswell of political activism across the nation in which various state legislatures took action to overturn earlier constitutional amendments and legalize same-sex marriage. Gov. Abercrombie, in consultation with the Senate president and the Speaker of the House, decided to call a special session of the legislature to pass a statute that would change the definition of marriage and allow same-sex couples to be married. The announcement about a special session caused a great deal of angst, hand-wringing and consternation in Hawai'i. Voices both for and against gay marriage were raised, often in shrill and strident tones.

I was involved in helping to shepherd the passage of such a bill through the legislature. Jill Nagamine, James Walther, Deirdre Marie-Iha and Anne Lopez, a small group of deputy attorneys general who called themselves "The Flaming Marrys," were principally involved in crafting and drafting legislation that would accomplish this goal. There were many drafts, as the team worked with the governor's team, various legislators and advocacy groups. The bill was crafted to allow some exemptions for religious persons such as priests and ministers to decline officiating at marriage ceremonies.

The Senate took the bill up first. The Senate Judiciary Committee allowed testimony from many people both for and against the bill. The committee hearing occurred in the large legislative auditorium room, rather than one of the smaller conference rooms, because of the many senators sitting in on the testimony and the large number of people testifying. I personally testified in favor of the bill before a number of legislative committees regarding what the bill did and didn't do, as well as how it addressed various related issues, such as religious freedom and the rights of clergy and others to refuse to engage in solemnization and other services ancillary to marriage ceremonies.

There were numerous courageous senators who spoke up in favor of the civil rights of same-sex couples, noting that it was simply a human right to choose to marry and live with a person that they loved. Senator Gil Kahele gave a memorable speech talking about the acceptance of mahu and same-sex relationships in Native Hawaiian culture. There were other senators who spoke against the bill, taking the side of the conservatives, the Catholic Church and other fundamentalist religious groups. The Senate quickly passed the bill by a large majority in a few days with a minimum of fuss.

The state House of Representatives appeared much more divided than the Senate on how it would deal with the bill. Hundreds of people signed up to testify, both for and against the bill. Representative Karl Rhoads, the House judiciary chair, also indicated that he would allow each person to speak for three minutes, which was longer than had been allowed in the Senate. The House proceedings thus became longer and more drawn out than the Senate proceedings. I also testified before the House committee. The hearing went on for days and days. The House committee members certainly had iron backsides as they listened to the voluminous testimony, some vocal, some emotional, some calm, some volatile. The House also had many representatives speak up and give their reasons for and against the bill. I was particularly moved by the speech of Representative Richard Onishi, who spoke eloquently that this was a simple matter of civil rights, equality and dignity.

There was a great deal of drama as this process unfolded. There were daily noisy, loud and occasionally raucous demonstrations and rallies in the State Capitol rotunda, right outside of the House and Senate chambers, both for and against the bill. Busloads of people on both sides came to bear witness to the process and demonstrate their opinions. There were bands and bullhorns, shouting and chanting. The media, both television and print, had extensive coverage of the special session and the demonstrations. There were numerous interviews with legislators, supporters and opponents explaining their reasoning, their feelings and their passionate views.

It was clear to me that the decision of Gov. Abercrombie to call a special session was the right one. The issue of same-sex marriage was so important, and yet so contentious, that it was critical for the issue to be considered separately, apart from the thousands of bills that normally are considered in a regular legislative session. A singularly important issue such as this needed to get the attention and consideration it deserved, without the distractions of other bills and the normal legislative time constraints. If this issue had come up in regular session, it might become the subject of horse trading and compromises on other bills and interests, or might simply be too contentious to pass. A special session allowed the legislature, for better or worse, to provide clarity of purpose and intent on this issue.

In the middle of all of this hoopla, I encountered one of the genuinely weirdest moments I ever had with a legislator. Someone once asked what the worst thing about my job as attorney general was. There is no question that dealing with a few of the legislators was absolutely the worst part of it. Don't get me wrong—most of the legislators I worked with were intelligent, straightforward, well-meaning and principled people. But there were also a few petty tyrants, bullies and uninformed but overconfident egos trying to get their way.

Gov. Abercrombie and I were invited to meet with the Republican caucus in the House to discuss the bill and various issues surrounding the bill. Republicans in Hawai'i are an endangered species. Since the events of the 1950s, Hawai'i has been a very Democratic state with strong union ties. There were six or seven Republicans in the House out of fifty-one representatives. There have been several Republican representatives who switched parties and became Democrats after being elected, realizing that they would be able to get more done as members of the majority caucus.

The governor and I were ushered into the Republican caucus room and began our conversation about the marriage equality bill. Predictably, the Republican caucus was almost universally against the idea of same-sex marriage. Only one of the Republican representatives was in favor of marriage equality. The others spent a great deal of time haranguing the governor and me, arguing that the bill was improper, the procedure of calling a special session was improper, same-sex marriage was immoral, etc.

The weirdest moment came when Richard Fale, one of the Republican representatives, took his turn to ask us questions. "Mr. Attorney General," he began, "I am the only elected person in all of the United States of Tongan ancestry, and because of that I take it upon myself to represent the interests of all Pacific Island people. Mr. Attorney General, wouldn't you agree that if not for the illegal overthrow of the Hawaiian kingdom in the 1880s by the United States government, we would not even have to think about or entertain the purely Western concept of same-sex marriage for Hawai'i, and that we should not do so now?"

This question and statement was stunning in their absurdity, ignorance and hypocrisy. I understood that Fale was a devout Mormon, who wore his religion on his sleeve. The Mormon religion was and is a completely Western concept that Fale had embraced wholeheartedly, and yet here he was, trying to assert that Western concepts had no place in Hawai'i. He was trying to posit that the Native Hawaiian sovereignty movement was antithetical to the issue of same-sex marriage. Moreover, he was simply wrong about same-sex relationships being a "Western" concept and having no place in Hawai'i. Ancient Hawaiians had allowed for and respected homosexual relationships as embodied by mahu. Senator Kahele, a Native Hawaiian, had already made a floor speech noting this very history.

These thoughts went through my mind as I framed my response. I wanted to be polite, since Representative Fale was theoretically a client of the attorney general. So I began by saying that I disagreed with him that same-sex relationships were a purely Western concept, noting that such relationships were both common and respected in Hawaiian culture. I also told him that the overthrow of the Hawaiian kingdom had nothing to do with the constitutional issues of equal protection under the law and according dignity to same-sex couples.

When I paused, Gov. Abercrombie cut to the chase. "Young man," he said, addressing Fale, "you took an oath to uphold the constitutions of the United States and Hawai'i. I have been doing that in my career for the past five decades, and I suggest that you start doing so now yourself." Fale had nothing to say.

The bill passed both houses of the legislature. As they say, timing is everything. We were at a momentous point in Hawai'i's history and the history of the United States. It was an opportunity to do the right thing, to provide equality, to bring people out of the shadows into the light. Fifteen years before, a number of courageous Hawai'i legislators had similarly taken a stand in favor of same-sex marriage and had been voted out of office for their views. This time around, the culture and understanding of both the nation and Hawai'i had changed, so there were no such repercussions.

Gov. Abercrombie had a big ceremony to sign the bill into law. The governor read from a letter from a family friend, "'Finally—today, now—all those who have been invisible will be visible to themselves and the whole world.'" He brought Nina Baehr to witness the signing and gave her one of the pens he used that officially made the bill into law. It was moving. I was proud and gratified to have been part of the effort.

But we were not done. Almost immediately, House representative Bob McDermott filed a lawsuit challenging the new law and seeking an injunction to prevent it from going into effect, claiming that it was unconstitutional. I had the privilege of arguing the motion in court for the State to defend the new law. The trial court gave due consideration to the arguments of the plaintiff and then dismissed the case, finding that the law was constitutional. The ruling was appealed and the lawsuit continued on for several years, finally getting a hearing before the Hawai'i Supreme Court in December 2014, after I had left the office. The Hawai'i Supreme Court upheld the ruling by the lower court and the power of the legislature to legalize same-sex marriage. The battle over the law for marriage equality in Hawai'i was finished. Hawai'i, after a long hiatus, had finally done the right thing to recognize that gay and lesbian people were not second-class citizens and should be accorded the dignity and respect that heterosexual couples enjoyed.

Since that time, Hawai'i has not been a battleground over these issues, but the culture wars regarding the acceptance of gay and lesbian couples have continued in other states. Courts have continued to rule on conduct regarding these issues. In Kentucky, marriage licenses were denied to gay and lesbian couples by a government clerk who claimed she did not have to follow the law. She was later removed from office. In Colorado, a bakery was cited for discriminating against a gay couple who wanted to purchase a wedding cake. That case went to the United States Supreme Court, which held that the governmental proceedings upholding the citation were flawed.

The continuing issue primarily seems to be whether people can discriminate against same-sex couples based upon the subjective claim that they are exercising their rights of religious freedom, which is impossible to prove or disprove. Undoubtedly, there will be more battles in the future, as a change in the law does not always result in a change in the hearts and minds of people. But I felt, and was proud of the fact, that we were on the right side of history with what we had done. ❦

| 7 |

Legacy of a Kingdom Past

Some of the most fascinating and complex legal issues that crossed my desk as attorney general involved Native Hawaiians. Hawai'i has a unique history. It was once a kingdom, populated by native, indigenous people, that was illegally overthrown with the help of the United States, then became a territory of the United States, and later, a state. The echoes of that history and the manner in which Hawai'i became a state reverberate today and affect many legal, political and social considerations for the people and the State. It is said that the past is prologue. Although native, indigenous Hawaiians are not now the majority of the people in Hawai'i, the 2019 US Census Bureau data shows that about 10.1% of Hawai'i's population identifies as Native Hawaiian or other Pacific Islander when people identify as only one race, but that 27% of the population identifies as such when people identify as having two or more races or ethnicities. Hawaiians and people who identify as being part Hawaiian thus comprise a significant segment of the population and the community.

More importantly, since the overthrow of the kingdom of Hawai'i, and similar to the history of other indigenous peoples, Hawaiians have often been treated poorly and have not shared in the bounty and riches derived by others from the resources of the islands. There has been and continues to be a palpable sense of injustice, dispossession, disenfranchisement and neglect visited upon the Hawaiian people in their own land.

It was in the context of this history that I had the privilege and responsibility as attorney general to analyze and deal with a number of important legal issues relating to Hawaiians. These were some of the same legislative issues we had to weigh when considering our legal strategy in the *Jackson* case about same-sex marriage. The genesis of these issues regarding Hawaiians had occurred long before my time, and the issues were complicated and overlaid with the weight of history. The State has been dealing with legal issues concerning Hawaiians for many, many years, and there are prior Hawai'i Supreme Court as well as United States Supreme Court decisions addressing some issues. But the courts have not provided definitive guidance on all matters. Issues involving Hawaiians often are simultaneously legal and political, raising constitutional questions, with historical and cultural dimensions, sometimes without much precedent.

These legal issues are complex, not just because of the history involved, but because many questions require political rather than legal solutions as a way to achieve reconciliation of past wrongs as well as a path forward. As with many issues that have political, cultural and historical dimensions, the tools of lawyers and legal solutions play an important part, though they do not always provide the answers needed. But those were the tools I had.

The legal issues that came to me regarding Native Hawaiians raised three fundamental questions that go to the heart of the purpose and structure of government, as well as to the tension between fundamental values enshrined in the United States and Hawai'i constitutions. First, when should the courts defer to the political process for solutions? There is a dynamic tension between the courts and the legislature in many areas, including Hawaiian issues. The courts want to make sure that justice is done, and sometimes they are disappointed and frustrated by the slowness of legislators and politicians to deal with pressing as well as long-standing problems. Yet the political process, with a four-year gubernatorial and state senatorial cycle and a two-year cycle for the House, does not always lend itself to thoughtful, well-reasoned and comprehensive solutions. Still, this is the democratic process that we have for making policy. It is the role of the legislature, not the courts, to make policy. Some questions and issues are best left to this political process rather than the courts, although the courts do have a role to play, as lawsuits are filed by people frustrated with the slowness of the political process.

Second, how are Hawaiian issues involving preferences and remedial actions to be addressed in accordance with the equal protection principles set forth in the constitutions and subsequent case law? Although the Fourteenth Amendment was originally secured to protect the rights of Blacks and other minority groups, in past decades there has been a significant amount of United States Supreme Court case law which has struck down affirmative action initiatives, racial preferences and other remedial actions in the name of equal protection.

Third, what are the fundamental powers and attributes inherent in governments, and should the sovereign power of the State be adjusted to accommodate a Hawaiian government entity, which might be created or recognized by the United States government to address and redress historical wrongs?

There are few legal guideposts or definitive United States or Hawai'i Supreme Court decisions to provide easy answers to these and other questions. Smart, intelligent and committed lawyers can always find support both for and against their positions in prior court opinions. There are always general principles, but the devil is always in the details. My job was to try and evaluate the situations and apply the law as best I could.

My approach to these issues was both personal and professional. Given my personal background, I felt that it was important to support Hawaiian programs and initiatives as much as possible, as part of a broader historical and social effort to, in some way, make up for injustices of long ago. In addition to my personal preferences, I had an obligation to determine what was required under the law, to try to find the best way forward consistent with the principles set forth in the constitutions. Moreover, while I believe it is important to try to address historical wrongs, I also firmly believe that for issues of governing, we always have to deal with the practical reality of the situation that exists now. The reality to me was that Hawai'i does not exist in a vacuum. It is one of the states of the Union, with many varied, diverse and productive citizens whose wants, needs and desires all had to be taken into account, so that issues regarding Hawaiians also had to be considered within the context of what is best for everyone.

I believed then and still believe that in dealing with these issues, care must be taken because of the history of social injustice and the realization that decisions and actions taken today will affect and shape the future relationship of the State and the Hawaiian people. My goal in dealing with Hawaiian issues was to try and make progress, try to move the ball forward, even if just a little bit, knowing that a comprehensive solution was not likely at hand, but also believing that by helping to realize some progress, a foundation could be laid for perhaps larger and more comprehensive solutions in the future. These factors made the job unique.

Legacy

In order to understand the legal matters relating to Hawaiians that I dealt with as attorney general, it is important to understand some of the history of Hawaiʻi. Although I was not raised in Hawaiʻi, in my years of living here I had absorbed some of that history. But I still had a lot to learn, which required research to understand the legal issues and how Hawaiʻi had gotten to this juncture. The following is a brief summary of some historical points to provide context for the matters I dealt with.

For centuries before contact by Captain Cook and Europeans in the 1770s, Hawaiʻi was populated by a native indigenous people of Polynesian descent. It is important to note that in Hawaiʻi, the term "Hawaiian" means to refer to such people. This is different from the common usage of a word including a state name to describe people who live in the state, such as "Californian," "Texan" or "Oregonian." In Hawaiʻi, a "Hawaiian" is not someone who simply lives in or is from the state. Instead, the terms "Hawaiian" or "Native Hawaiian" with a capital *N* refer to all people of indigenous Hawaiian ancestry. The term "native Hawaiian" using an uncapitalized *n* is a legal term from the Hawaiian Homes Commission Act (HHCA) that means people who have 50% or more Hawaiian ancestry by blood quantum.

The kingdom of Hawaiʻi came into being in 1795, when Kamehameha the Great unified the Hawaiian Islands. The kingdom entered into treaties and conventions with many other nations, including the United States, recognizing its independence. There was also a long history of missionaries and settlers coming from the United States to live in Hawaiʻi. The kingdom welcomed and allowed non-Hawaiians to settle and participate in the society and the government. But this welcoming attitude had consequences.

As the kingdom grew and the economy flourished, large sugar and pineapple plantations arose, and many settlers and businessmen wanted more control and wanted Hawaiʻi to be part of the United States. In 1887, a group of white businessmen and lawyers forced King David Kalākaua at gunpoint to sign the Bayonet Constitution, which significantly reduced the power of the monarchy, gave most of the power to the legislature, made the king little more than a figurehead and deprived most Native Hawaiians of their voting rights.

When the United States Congress passed the Tariff Act of 1890, it ended the favored status of sugar imported from Hawaiʻi and raised import rates on foreign sugar, crippling Hawai'i's sugar industry. This caused many businessmen and politicians to seriously consider overthrowing the monarchy so that Hawai'i could be annexed by the United States. Annexation would give Hawai'i sugar growers the same rates as other United States producers and restore profitability.

In 1891, Queen Lili'uokalani ascended to the throne upon the death of King Kalākaua and sought a new constitution to restore the power of the monarchy. In 1893, a small group of white businessmen and settlers, including citizens and agents of the United States, decided to overthrow the kingdom and obtained the complicity of the United States minister to the kingdom in this endeavor. The overthrow by military force was protested by Queen Lili'uokalani in a moving letter to President Grover Cleveland. Her protests were to no avail, and Lili'uokalani abdicated the throne to avoid the bloodshed of her people.

The illegal overthrow of the Hawaiian kingdom by white businessmen, with the support of the United States government, is a shameful chapter in the history of the United States. The group established a provisional government, which then became the Republic of Hawai'i. In 1898, the United States Congress passed the Newlands Joint Resolution, which annexed Hawai'i to the United States. Upon annexation, the Republic ceded and transferred 1.8 million acres of public, government and crown lands to the United States. These lands are known as the "ceded" lands. In 1900, Congress passed the Organic Act, which established and defined the political structure and powers of a government for the territory of Hawai'i.

Hawaiians had not done well over the years and under the new government. In 1920, after holding hearings and determining that Hawaiians were a "dying race," with the number of "full-blooded Hawaiians" dropping from 142,650 in 1826 to 22,600 in 1919, Congress enacted the HHCA, which mandated that approximately 200,000 acres of the ceded lands be permanently held in trust for the benefit of "native Hawaiians." The HHCA was intended to address the decline of "the Hawaiian race" by providing "lands and the mode of living that their ancestors were accustomed to." The lands could not be sold, but Hawaiians could obtain homesteads and occupy the land under long-term leases.

However, the goals of the program were hampered for two reasons. Although Prince Jonah Kūhiō Kalaniana'ole of Hawai'i spearheaded the effort and sought to make the program widely available to Hawaiians with 1/32 blood ancestry, the HHCA defined "native Hawaiians" as only those with 50% blood ancestry, thus greatly reducing the number of eligible people. In addition, many of the lands included in this grant were rocky, marginal lands, without water, so they were not particularly valuable or useful for agriculture or economic development. Nonetheless, the HHCA was important because it acknowledged the trust responsibility of the United States to the Hawaiian people.

In 1959, Hawai'i became the fiftieth state of the Union. Congress passed the Admission Act, which gave the State title to most of the ceded lands. As a condition of admission, the State agreed to hold the ceded lands in a public land trust, with the revenues from those lands to be used for five purposes, including the betterment of the conditions of native Hawaiians as defined in the HHCA. The State was also required to adopt the HHCA as part of its constitution. The Department of Hawaiian Home Lands (DHHL) is the formal department of the State that administers the HHCA.

When I first came to Hawai'i in 1976, I observed many efforts and actions to foster a renaissance and resurgence of Hawaiian culture. There were many Hawaiian music groups, hula groups and a growing emphasis on recognizing and using the Hawaiian language, both in the media and officially in the government. Such efforts have been very successful over the past several decades.

In 1978, a constitutional convention was held to review Hawai'i's constitution and consider whether changes should be made. The new constitution established the Office of Hawaiian Affairs (OHA) as a semiautonomous, self-governing state agency, with a mandate to better the conditions of the Hawaiian community. The convention also recognized that the DHHL had historically been underfunded and included a provision requiring "sufficient" funding for DHHL.

Beginning in the 1970s, there was also a growing awareness of self-determination and political power for Hawaiian interests and causes. Protests and demonstrations occurred against the use of the island of Kaho'olawe by the United States Navy as a bombing target. Those efforts were successful, and the Navy stopped using the island as a bombing target in 1990 and transferred it to the state in 1994. Protests and demonstrations in 1977 also stopped the development of houses and a golf course on 600 acres in the Waiāhole and Waikāne valleys on O'ahu that had been traditional agricultural areas inhabited by Hawaiians. In 1993, the US Congress passed the Apology Resolution, which apologized for the role of the US in overthrowing the Hawaiian monarchy.

The idea of Hawaiian sovereignty, the establishment and recognition of a separate Hawaiian form of government, has been extensively discussed for many years. Senator Daniel Akaka proposed bills in Congress to provide a process for federal recognition of a Hawaiian government, similar to the recognition of Native American Indian tribal governments. However, such bills did not pass, and Hawaiian sovereignty remains an elusive concept, although the idea continues to be discussed.

How the State and the people of Hawai'i deal with Hawaiians is a dynamic and constantly evolving issue. Hawaiians are the indigenous people of Hawai'i, and yet are a minority in their own land. What is the obligation of the State to the Hawaiian people? How much money should be made available by the State to DHHL to develop homesteads for native Hawaiians? How much money from ceded lands revenues should be given to OHA? What are the practical realities of law enforcement and regulation if a Hawaiian government is established? These and other questions regarding Hawaiian issues have yet to be resolved.

There are many who believe that the State has not lived up to its obligations to the Hawaiian people over the years since statehood. At the same time, there have been those who for ideological reasons have actively sought to challenge and block any State action, preferences or programs to benefit Hawaiians. Lawsuits have been filed on both sides to either enhance and improve State programs for Hawaiians or to restrict and do away with such programs, claiming that these are unconstitutional preferences. This was the backdrop for my involvement in legal issues relating to Hawaiians.

Monies Claimed by the Office of Hawaiian Affairs

One of the larger issues involving Hawaiians I became involved in was dealing with and settling claims by OHA against the State that had been outstanding and a bone of contention for over thirty years. Since 1980, OHA had claimed that additional monies were owed to it for ceded lands revenues. In 2011, OHA believed that it was owed approximately $400 million, although others believed it was much larger.

In 1980, the legislature enacted a law that 20% of all "funds" from ceded lands should go to OHA. The State and OHA disagreed as to what this meant and how much money was owed, resulting in a lawsuit. The Hawai'i Supreme Court eventually held that "funds" was not sufficiently defined, so the courts could not resolve the dispute. In response, in 1990 the legislature amended the statute to provide that 20% of all "revenue" from ceded lands should go to OHA. But this was still not sufficiently clear, since monies involving ceded lands are generated in many different ways, and the parties continued to disagree.

OHA and the State entered into a $129 million settlement in 1993 over some, but not all of the claims. The devil is always in the details. Some of the remaining claims included whether "revenue" included monies from sales at luxury "duty-free" stores at the airport and in Waikīkī (based on the lease of ceded lands at the airport, although federal regulations prohibited payment of revenues for non-airport purposes); Hilo Hospital patient receipts, because the hospital was on ceded lands; receipts from state agencies for low-cost housing projects located on ceded lands; and interest on unpaid sums.

Unsuccessful attempts to settle these claims had previously been made during the administrations of both Gov. Ben Cayetano and Gov. Linda Lingle. In 1999, Gov. Cayetano offered $251 million and 360,000 acres of ceded lands to resolve all past and future claims, but OHA refused. In 2008, OHA and the State agreed to settle the past claims for $200 million in cash or a combination of land and cash, but the legislature did not approve. The settlement had to be approved by the legislature, because state law prohibits the transfer of any state land without legislative approval by a two-thirds vote. This law prevents the State administration from improvidently giving away lands and allows the legislature to make sure that any proposed State land transfers are fully vetted and considered.

There were several factors that seemed to scuttle previous deals. Some of the proposals sought a global final settlement over all claims, both past and future, but many in the Hawaiian community were opposed to giving up future rights. Many Hawaiians came out to testify against the proposed settlement in 2008, claiming that they had not been consulted and that there was a lack of transparency in the settlement process. Some people objected to the quality of the lands that were proposed to be given to OHA, which included prime property in the heart of downtown Honolulu near the waterfront as well as hotel property in Hilo and industrial property in West O'ahu. Others simply wanted OHA to hold out for a better deal. Finally, because Gov. Lingle was a Republican in a largely Democratic state, there was a question whether the legislature was inclined to assist a Republican administration in the resolution of a major initiative involving Hawaiians. The legislature failed to approve the deal in both the 2008 and 2010 legislative sessions.

Shortly after I assumed office in 2011, I was contacted by William Meheula, a prominent attorney of Hawaiian descent whom I had known for many years and who had represented OHA in prior attempts at settlement. Did we want to try and settle the claims and get legislative approval? I worked with Charleen Aina, a senior deputy attorney general and a Native Hawaiian who had been involved in working on the OHA settlement, to see what we could do to resurrect the deal and move forward. Aina was very knowledgeable about Hawaiian issues and provided thoughtful analysis on this issue and other important litigation involving Hawaiians.

It was clear to me that following through on a settlement of these claims would be a good thing. It would resolve long-standing grievances that were thirty years old and a sore point in relations between the Hawaiian community and the State, fostering some healing which might become the basis for future agreements. It was also clear that there was no money in the State coffers to fund a settlement. Hawai'i and the nation were still in the throes of the so-called Great Recession dating back to 2008. Tax revenues were still down, and there were large budget deficits.

Because there was no money, the only way to settle such large claims was to give OHA land, not money. It was also my view that settlements have a better chance of being agreed to when there are less, not more, moving parts. To get a settlement that would receive legislative approval, I thought we needed to simplify the terms and address the criticisms that had arisen before.

The first question was how much to settle for. The claims sought approximately $400 million. But there were a number of valid defenses that put such claims at risk and made them uncertain. OHA might prevail in court, but the State also might prevail, so there was risk for both sides. Additionally, it would take years to have the issues decided by the courts. $200 million seemed like a good approximate assessment of the risk to the State, and we knew that OHA had agreed to that number before.

Another question was whether we would try for a global final settlement and the curtailment and release of all future OHA claims. As discussions on this issue had proved contentious in the past and had engendered substantial opposition, I thought we should simply try to resolve the past claims in order to get them off the table, clear the slate and leave the resolution of future claims for another day.

The next question was what lands should we offer OHA? We already knew that there had been objections to the quality of some of the lands previously offered. Since the legislature had already rejected the OHA settlement once, we wanted to address as many objections as we could, to improve the chances of legislative approval.

I met with Gov. Abercrombie to discuss a potential settlement. The law gives the attorney general the power to control and make decisions about all litigation involving the State, but it requires the attorney general to consult with the governor on all significant litigation. Gov. Abercrombie understood the historic nature of the issues and was in favor of getting these matters resolved. Indeed, decades before as a state senator, Gov. Abercrombie had predicted that there would be continuing recriminations and arguments over how much money should be paid to OHA.

As we discussed possible lands to give to OHA, it also became clear that there were not that many lands that could make the list. While the State has a lot of land throughout the islands, much of that land was already in use, either through one of the departments or through leases to other government entities or third parties. In downtown Honolulu, the Kaka'ako Makai (*makai* means on the ocean side) area was one of the last large undeveloped areas of land. While some development had occurred there, many of the parcels were still vacant and were simply being used as parking lots. The Hilo hotel property and West O'ahu industrial property previously offered to OHA did not seem to have as much development potential as Kaka'ako Makai. Together, Gov. Abercrombie and I came up with the concept of giving OHA only parcels in the Kaka'ako Makai area, as those would be the most attractive lands and possibly reduce objections by Hawaiians.

Because these lands were in the heart of downtown Honolulu, they were already quite valuable, so they had a high value per square foot. Less acreage of such high-value parcels would need to be given to OHA to reach an approximate $200 million valuation. Also, prime real estate in the heart of Honolulu would likely appreciate, become more valuable and provide an income stream to assist OHA in furthering its mission. In my view, the State had time on its side. On a long-term basis, eventually the State's other lands would become valuable. But in the short run, giving up valuable land in downtown Honolulu would get the job accomplished without a big sacrifice to the State.

Through my prior experience with the Aloha Tower Development Corporation (ATDC), the state agency charged with developing the area around Aloha Tower, I had learned that for the State to do any significant development requires substantial political capital and will. I did not think that the State would have the political will or capital to put together any major developments in the Kakaʻako Makai area any time soon. Because of existing restrictions against residential development in Kakaʻako Makai resulting from prior community protests, there was even a question whether successful development in the area could be achieved. The development consultants for ATDC had repeatedly stressed that successful developments require a mixed-use combination of residential, business and government infrastructure.

Gov. Abercrombie was already using his political capital and skills to move forward with plans to allow significant residential development in the nearby former light industrial area of Kakaʻako Mauka (*mauka* means on the mountain side) to address the large unmet need for housing in Honolulu. Even desperately needed housing projects in the area had opposition, mostly from people who already lived in some of the few residential developments in the Kakaʻako Mauka area but did not want further development.

Kakaʻako Makai had been under state jurisdiction ever since statehood but had only partially been developed. Many projects, such as a community center, had been talked about but had never been brought to fruition. Putting up a large government project would cost substantial money and without accompanying mixed-use development would likely mean that it would just be an expensive white elephant, only occasionally used. I did not think a government project in Kakaʻako Makai would be likely if the State had to push it forward.

However, I was hopeful that OHA might be able to develop some properties in the area that would be beneficial both to itself and the larger community. OHA could seek to develop projects that would enhance Hawaiian culture and community, as well as provide tourism offerings. Perhaps OHA, with its mission to benefit Hawaiians, could overcome public opposition and restrictions on residential development in Kakaʻako Makai. This would make those parcels much more valuable and enhance prospects for a successful mixed-use development. The idea was that OHA might be more nimble than the State in creating the elements for successful development. Both Kakaʻako Makai and Kakaʻako Mauka came under the jurisdiction of the Hawaiʻi Community Development Authority (HCDA), which regulated development, so the State would still have some control over OHA's use of the lands.

Another question was whether to settle for a specific number and have a cash payment (either by the State or OHA) to make up any difference between the tax-assessed property values and the settlement number. Neither the State nor OHA had any money to account for the difference. We decided to offer OHA specific parcels of land only in Kaka'ako Makai that were valued at close to $200 million, but without any cash component. The properties would be offered as-is, where-is, without any promises as to value, apart from the existing tax assessments. By offering only high value, prime properties in Kaka'ako Makai, I thought that this could make up for any concerns about not having an exact $200 million settlement.

OHA agreed to the deal we proposed. Of course, we both then had to sell the settlement to the Hawaiian community and the legislature. Getting support for any settlement from Hawaiian community organizations was critical, but we left this piece of the puzzle to OHA. OHA undertook to hold public meetings with the Hawaiian community, since it would appear self-serving for the State to appear and argue the reasonableness of the settlement in such forums. OHA held many such meetings and was successful in getting community support.

Both the State and OHA then had to sell the deal to the legislature. As described in the chapter on marriage equality, we had to make some compromises in how we handled a lawsuit about same-sex marriage in order to move the OHA settlement forward. In addition, we tried to address any concerns the legislature had about the settlement. Working with Meheula and OHA, we were successful in getting legislative approval.

After all of the hard work of documenting the deal, a ceremony to mark the settlement was held at Washington Place, the governor's ceremonial mansion. OHA chairperson Colette Machado gave a moving speech about how we had been able to put our differences behind us and come together to resolve long-standing differences. She specifically recognized the achievements of Charleen Aina in helping to push this forward. Gov. Abercrombie spoke about the historic nature of the settlement and praised the cooperation that had led us to this moment.

I was pleased to have been a part of the endeavor and to have helped push this settlement over the goal line. Because there was so much history involved with the OHA claims, which were only a small part of larger issues of social justice and reconciliation, I thought it important to resolve these claims without protracted court proceedings. Litigating in court would take years, or even decades, a process that would not be satisfying to anyone and could exacerbate tensions and resentments. These claims have cried out for a political, rather than legal solution, but the legislature did not appear likely to provide a comprehensive solution at any time soon to the many Hawaiian issues that exist. Other political leaders in the past had tried and failed to achieve such a solution. Consequently, it fell to us to craft a settlement that could be approved by the legislature and resolve some, but not all, of the many existing claims.

Yet even as we celebrated this legal and political achievement, we knew that this was only a small piece of a complicated jigsaw puzzle, and that there were still other unresolved issues affecting Hawaiians that would require continuous attention and care.

| 8 |

More Echoes from the Past, Issues for the Future

Seeking to achieve progress and solutions regarding complex historical, political and legal matters is no simple matter. While I was pleased to participate in the Office of Hawaiian Affairs settlement, there were a host of other pressing and important Hawaiian matters that came before me as attorney general. Many of these involved both the past and the potential for significant change. As with the OHA issue, they were complex, dynamic and fraught with history. Some were political issues woven into the very fabric of Hawai'i's constitution, such as issues involving the Department of Hawaiian Home Lands (DHHL). Some were long-standing lawsuits that had begun before my time and would continue well after my time. Some were both echoes of past actions taken and a harbinger of things to come, such as the complex issue of Hawaiian sovereignty. All were unique and involved deep questions of how best to respect the indigenous Hawaiian people and culture, yet forge a path forward for all the people in Hawai'i.

I wanted to try to achieve some solutions, but the complexity of many of these issues precluded easy answers. Sometimes I could contribute by helping to create a small solution. Other times it appeared that there was no consensus or clear path on how to proceed, so that resolution would have to wait. The following is a recap of some of the matters we dealt with to give you, the reader, a sense of the scope and complicated nature of these issues and challenges.

The Department of Hawaiian Home Lands

The DHHL presents a host of complex legal, political and social issues to the State. I was involved in analyzing and taking positions on some of these issues. While DHHL has an obligation and opportunity to do positive things for native Hawaiians, it also has a daunting task with huge challenges. Like any other landowner who is land rich and cash poor, DHHL historically has had to figure out how to fulfill its mandate with limited resources, using lands that were in many instances not particularly valuable or suited for development. DHHL has also been dependent upon the executive and legislative branches of government to obtain funding for its mission and for hiring staff. Additionally, the challenge of fulfilling DHHL's mandate has had to be accomplished within the strictures of the Hawaiian Homes Commission Act (HHCA), which was enacted by Congress in the 1920s under very different circumstances than are present today. The US Department of the Interior has oversight to ensure that DHHL adheres to the HHCA.

Congress had the idea that giving native Hawaiians homestead properties, as a piece of the pie, would help them to accumulate wealth, prosper and succeed. DHHL provides direct benefits to native Hawaiians in the form of ninety-nine-year homestead leases (since extended to 199 years) at an annual rent of $1. Although the goals of this program are laudable, a number of the structural aspects of this program have led to conflicts and issues not easily resolved.

Because homestead leases are economically quite desirable, there has been and still is a tremendous backlog of Hawaiians who have applied for homesteads but have not gotten them. The limited number of available homesteads and a long waiting list are a bad combination. This has frustrated and disappointed many who have applied and unsuccessfully waited for decades to get a homestead. The *Kalima v. State* lawsuit described below is a direct result of this problem. Additionally, over the years there has been a history of leases or land swaps sometimes being provided to insiders or on sweetheart terms.

One significant problem is that the DHHL lands available for homesteads have not always been the best lands. Some of the lands were prime lands, but others were less than desirable. Some of these lands were located in remote, rocky and rural areas, far away from roads, water and electricity. Such lands were better suited for grazing or agricultural pursuits than for housing.

Another problem has been that the mandate to carry out the mission of the HHCA taken on by the State upon statehood has been unfunded. The DHHL has historically not had the necessary funds to build and maintain infrastructure to make such lands suitable for housing in large numbers to meet demand. Building roads, sewers, sidewalks, street lights, electricity and plumbing to create housing developments is very expensive. Maintaining such infrastructure is also potentially expensive. Unless infrastructure meets county standards, the counties are reluctant to take over and maintain the infrastructure as they normally do with other private developments.

Because DHHL can only charge $1 per year in annual rent, homesteads do not generate any revenues that can be used to pay the process forward and create more homesteads. Hundreds of thousands of dollars can easily be spent for roads, sewers and modern infrastructure to support homestead development, but DHHL cannot recoup any of those monies from the homesteaders. Instead, any funds for infrastructure, improvements and maintenance have to come either from the State or from revenues derived from general leasing, i.e., long-term leases of larger parcels of property, not homesteads. Yet because many of the lands were not urban or highly valuable, the amount of revenue to be raised by leases has historically not been high. Thus, the program has always been in financial need to carry out its mission.

One situation came before me that illustrated these problems. Repairs needed to be done for sewer infrastructure in the Papakōlea district, a DHHL homesteading area within a mile of downtown Honolulu. Many decades ago, roads and sewers were built to support numerous homesteads where houses were built. The sewers connected to the sewers of the City & County of Honolulu but were not built to county standards and had never been dedicated to or accepted by the county. After decades of use, repairs needed to be made. Who would pay for and be responsible for such repairs, now and in the future? The obvious answer is that the county was in the best position to do that. The county had an agency in charge of sewers and experience in maintaining such, while DHHL had none. But the county was reluctant to accept liability for the Papakōlea sewers that were not built to county standards. Bringing such sewers up to county standards would require expensive remedial construction. I was disappointed we were not able to resolve this problem during my tenure.

Another issue we considered was the tension arising from the HHCA requirement established by Congress in the 1920s that homestead leases could only go to native Hawaiians with a minimum 50% of Hawaiian blood quantum, and if the original lessee passed away, to certain successors (spouse, children or grandchildren) with 25% Hawaiian blood.

These restrictions meant that if the deceased lessee had married a spouse or adopted children with less than 25% Hawaiian blood, they could not succeed to the family homestead. This seems hugely out of step with modern concepts of family and inheritance law, especially given the significant amount of racial intermarriages of Hawaiians and the Hawaiian tradition of *hānai* (adoption).

This issue confronts DHHL now and will do so in the future. One hundred years ago, blood quantum as a criteria was not unusual, and was one of the ways that governments dealt with people of color. But today, with so much racial intermarriage, especially in Hawaiʻi, the idea of blood quantum as the measure of whether or not a person is Hawaiian may no longer be appropriate. The trouble with using blood quantum is that, as time goes by and love and racial intermarriage occurs, the amount of Hawaiian blood in the next generation may be decreased. If a Native Hawaiian with 50% ancestry marries a non-Hawaiian, the children will have 25% blood quantum. Succeeding generations may have even less and may not meet the HHCA restrictions. DHHL and the Department of the Attorney General have previously raised this issue with the United States Department of the Interior to seek solutions and possible changes in policy. Yet this requirement can only be changed with the consent of Congress. Given the current political gridlock in Congress, it is questionable whether this issue will be addressed any time soon.

There were two significant court cases involving DHHL that were ongoing when I became attorney general. *Nelson v. Hawaiian Homes Commission* was a lawsuit brought in 2007 by several individuals against the State and DHHL, alleging that the State and the legislature had failed to appropriate "sufficient sums" as required by the Hawaiʻi Constitution to fund the operations of DHHL. Although DHHL was a defendant, since the goal of the suit was to increase DHHL's annual appropriations, DHHL was represented by separate outside legal counsel rather than the attorney general and was generally aligned against the State.

The *Nelson* case raised the issue of whether legislative appropriations are a "political question" that should be decided only by the legislature as a matter of policy, rather than by the courts. The plaintiffs and DHHL sought a ruling that the phrase "sufficient sums" in the Hawaiʻi Constitution required that large sums of money amounting to several tens of millions of dollars had to be appropriated each year to DHHL, and the courts could determine what was reasonable and sufficient. We argued on behalf of the State that only the legislature could make these determinations, and that the 1978 Constitutional Convention debate, which added this phrase to the constitution, at best referred to the 1978 appropriations of $1.3 to $1.6 million, rather than giving unlimited authority to the courts to make or second-guess legislative appropriations.

In 2012, the Hawai'i Supreme Court decided in *Nelson* that the courts could rule and decide what constituted "sufficient" appropriations. The decision created a great deal of unhappiness at the legislature, which believed that the courts were overstepping their proper role and authority in seeking to tell the legislature how much money should be appropriated each year to a State department. Following the 2012 *Nelson* decision, numerous bills were introduced and continue to be introduced at the legislature each year seeking to restrict and at times curtail judicial authority and budgets, as an expression of apparent unhappiness with court rulings in *Nelson* and other cases.

A key component of any functioning democracy is an independent judiciary, which is not subject to political influence, so these bills have represented an incursion upon the independence of the courts. Thankfully, most of these bills have been deferred and not passed into law. Throughout my career I have been a strong proponent of judicial independence. However, I also understand and appreciate the point of view of the legislature. This dynamic tension between the courts and the legislature continues to this day.

After more proceedings following the 2012 ruling, the *Nelson* case again came before the Hawai'i Supreme Court. In 2018, the Court decided that although the courts could rule on whether "sufficient sums" had been appropriated, the only judicially manageable standard to be applied was the 1978 baseline of $1.3 to $1.6 million, adjusted for inflation. The trial court recently ruled in favor of the State, that the appropriations of $17 million annually to DHHL exceeded the 1978 baseline, adjusted for inflation.

The second important case involving DHHL is *Kalima v. State*, which is a class action filed against the State in 1999 involving 2,721 claimants, alleging that the State and DHHL breached their fiduciary trust responsibilities to HHCA beneficiaries by failing to timely process applications and award homestead leases. The lawsuit seeks many tens of millions of dollars in damages for individuals whose applications were allegedly mishandled. The lawsuit is based upon Hawai'i Revised Statutes (HRS) Chapters 673 and 674, two special laws that gave certain individual beneficiaries a prospective right to bring claims against the State for delays in receiving homesteads, and set up an administrative process through a legislative panel to adjudicate such claims, to be followed by judicial proceedings. The State argued that the claims were improperly brought and barred by sovereign immunity.

In 2006, the Hawai'i Supreme Court ruled that the beneficiaries could properly sue the State for breach of trust claims. The case was sent back to the trial court, which ruled in 2009 that the State had breached its duties as trustee and was liable for damages. During my time as attorney general, the case remained before the trial court on various legal and factual issues, including the lack of documentation to support the claims, disputes over the methodologies to be used to determine damages and various other points of contention. The trial court eventually ruled on various issues, including adopting a damages model to approximate damages for beneficiaries, rather than making hundreds or thousands of beneficiaries prove their actual damages claims. The case again went up on appeal. In 2020, the Hawai'i Supreme Court ruled that the trial court's damages model was appropriate. This paved the way for possible finding by the trial court of damages that may amount to many tens of millions of dollars or more. The case has been again sent back to the trial court for further proceedings and will likely continue on.

My involvement with the *Nelson* and *Kalima* cases gave me an appreciation of how complex societal problems have to be addressed at many levels of government in order to achieve lasting solutions, and of the advantages and disadvantages of the courts in grappling with and fashioning solutions for problems that have many legal, political and cultural aspects, such as those involving Hawaiian issues. One advantage is that the courts can provide final legal pronouncements that are enforceable. However, one disadvantage is that legal processes can take an exceedingly long time, especially in complicated matters. Another disadvantage is that because these claims arise out of the Hawai'i Constitution, and in *Kalima,* a special law enacted to address the problems of DHHL beneficiaries, there is very little precedent, so the issues are of first impression and lawyers for both sides can and will raise cogent arguments in support of their positions. Because of the importance of the issues to the State as well as to Hawaiians, many times a decision is needed from the Hawai'i Supreme Court, and sometimes even the US Supreme Court. Yet getting such decisions from the highest courts can take years, if not decades.

I spent some long hours meeting with the deputies handling these cases and trying to understand the legal and factual issues that lay beneath the surface. I wanted to know if there was a way to shortcut the litigation and settle these lawsuits. I was periodically briefed about developments and interim decisions by the judges involved. I even met with a TV reporter covering the *Kalima* case to discuss the positions of the parties and whether a settlement was possible. Unfortunately, I concluded that there was too much disagreement about basic facts, and with so little legal precedent, the parties were too far apart to achieve a settlement. Although this was not the analysis I had hoped for, given the differing positions of the parties, all we could do was to soldier on and await further rulings from the courts. Still, it was important that we tried to move the ball forward to some resolution.

Corboy v. Louie

Legal issues involving Hawaiian rights and preferences often end up in court. On one hand, OHA and DHHL seek to do what they can with the resources they are given. Hawaiian activists and commentators have frequently expressed frustration that the State does not do enough, and should do more, so that lawsuits have been filed to force the State and its departments to take certain actions. On the other hand, there are conservative people and groups who think the State has done too much and seek to block, prevent and dismantle such programs and any Hawaiian preferences. This latter position has given rise to lawsuits claiming that Hawaiian programs violate both the constitutions of the State of Hawai'i and the United States on equal protection grounds.

The backdrop and context for much of this litigation is the issue of whether preferences for people of color or racial groups may stand, even when they are intended to address and ameliorate discrimination and prejudice that occurred many decades or centuries ago. Set-asides in government for minority-owned businesses, affirmative action in higher education admissions and preferences in job hires for historically closed professions such as police and firefighters have all been the subject of continuing litigation across the nation. Should government and educational institutions reflect the diversity of the population? Should there be quotas or affirmative action? Should there be racial preferences, all things being equal?

For Hawaiians, the issue is complicated by the illegal overthrow of the kingdom of Hawai'i and the discrimination directed toward Hawaiians for many years, along with the mandates to benefit Hawaiians in the

Hawaiʻi Constitution. Is it appropriate for the State of Hawaiʻi to provide resources to Hawaiians as special designees for benefits? Others contend that government is supposed to function for the benefit of all of the people, so that preferences are unconstitutional. There are proponents and opponents on all sides of these issues, with deeply held views that can be polemic and contentious.

Corboy v. Louie was a lawsuit raising these issues that almost reached the United States Supreme Court for decision. Corboy was one of a group of plaintiffs supported by conservative groups who sought to challenge Hawaiian preferences as an ideological matter. The HHCA and DHHL were simply grist for their ideological mill.

The suit was originally brought against my predecessor, Mark Bennett, as the attorney general of Hawaiʻi, and bore his name, but when I came into office the caption was changed to substitute my name, since I was the officeholder, and it was the office that was being sued. I was strongly in favor of defending Native Hawaiian rights and programs. I thought this was important for Hawaiians, and was important in the larger context of addressing and remedying historical discrimination against people of color.

The *Corboy* case was nominally about real property tax exemptions, but it was really about challenging any preferences for Hawaiians on the grounds that they were unconstitutional. The HHCA gave Hawaiians who were original DHHL homestead lessees an exemption from all taxes for seven years of their leases. Conservative ideological groups and non-Hawaiians sued, claiming that the tax exemptions violated the Fourteenth Amendment as a racial preference. The State argued that the tax exemptions were not unconstitutional, did not involve race, only the status of being a homestead lessee, and that plaintiffs did not have "standing" since they had not sought to become homestead lessees.

The Hawaiʻi Supreme Court ruled in 2011 that plaintiffs did not have standing. Standing is an important gatekeeping legal doctrine that governs who can bring a lawsuit on a given issue and focuses on whether the plaintiff has a personal stake or suffered damage to justify the exercise of the court's powers. In other words, a plaintiff has to establish that they have personally been injured, not just that they are airing a political or intellectual grievance.

Many battles over important legal issues such as equal protection have been resolved and decided not on the merits, but instead on procedural issues such as standing. Standing has been applied as a doctrine to block various challenges to Hawaiian preferences and programs. In *Corboy*, the Hawai'i Supreme Court held that because none of the plaintiffs had applied for a homestead lease, they did not have any injury or damage that would give them standing to bring the claims. Of course, because this case involved constitutional questions, this ruling did not definitively end the case. The *Corboy* plaintiffs sought review before the United States Supreme Court, seeking certiorari, which is the Supreme Court's process for deciding which cases it will take.

This now raised an interesting personal question: If the case made it to the United States Supreme Court's docket, should I argue it? Arguing before the Supreme Court is, for many lawyers, the pinnacle of success. It is the World Series and Super Bowl of legal proceedings. Would you turn down the chance to pitch in the World Series if it was offered to you? As the attorney general directing the litigation, and since the case even bore my name, it was my decision to make. My predecessor, Mark J. Bennett, argued two cases before the Supreme Court. Other state attorneys general have argued before the "Supremes," sometimes to mixed reviews.

I thought about this briefly and talked to others who had argued before the Supreme Court. Despite my desire to argue at the highest levels, I felt that the issue was too important to the State, Native Hawaiians and Hawaiian programs to let my vanity dictate who would argue the case. I decided to hire counsel with expertise in Supreme Court practice. Charleen Aina and I interviewed several Supreme Court practitioners. We were even contacted by lawyers offering their services and looking to make a name for themselves. We eventually retained Carter Phillips, an experienced Supreme Court practitioner.

The first step was to write briefs to determine whether the Court should even take the case. The very best Supreme Court counsel are great writers who are able to take complex concepts, distill them to their essence and express their client's position clearly and elegantly. After the briefs were submitted, we met in Washington, DC, with Phillips and Sri Srinivasan, the principal deputy solicitor general of the United States (now a federal appeals court judge), to preview our arguments in what is called a CVSG, a call for the views of the solicitor general. The solicitor general handles all Supreme Court litigation, and has been called the "tenth Justice," because the nine Supreme Court justices often seek the solicitor general's view on pending cases.

Our meeting was happily successful. Later, the Supreme Court denied certiorari, which meant that the court refused to hear the case.

The case was over; the challenge to the HHCA had been rebuffed. I was pleased to have played a part in upholding Hawai'i's constitution, the HHCA and the general idea of Hawaiian programs, even if on technical grounds. Not all decisions of the Supreme Court have ended as well for Hawaiian programs.

Hawaiian Sovereignty

Before I came to Hawai'i, the Hawaiian sovereignty movement existed as a political and cultural campaign to establish a Hawaiian form of government, by and for Hawaiians. The movement, and issues of self-determination, self-governance and a form of government with land and funds, gained more traction and public acceptance in the 1980s and 1990s, with a variety of different organizations and positions. Some groups have sought to form a nation within a nation, similar to Native American tribal organizations. Other groups have advocated for an independent Hawaiian nation or kingdom. Some have favored state recognition; others favored federal recognition. I have not seen a consensus in the Hawaiian community regarding the form of a potential Hawaiian government, or how to achieve this goal.

Beginning in 2000, Senator Daniel Akaka proposed several bills in Congress for a federal process to recognize a Hawaiian government. Although some of the bills came close to passage, they were all unsuccessful. The Akaka Bill proposed federal recognition similar to that accorded Native American tribal governments. An earlier version of the bill had almost passed. It provided for negotiations and agreement between the State and the new Hawaiian governmental entity over how the two governments would work together as a precondition of federal recognition. However, the last version of the Akaka Bill proposed in 2010 eliminated that condition. Without such negotiations, the State might be subject to unwanted existing federal laws or decisions about the authority of such a new entity. Gov. Lingle and Attorney General Bennett withdrew their support of the Akaka Bill over that issue, and the bill died.

Most of the political and legal maneuvering regarding the Akaka Bill occurred before my tenure. However, the issue continued to be discussed at both the state and national levels. Although I was not called upon to take any formal actions or positions as attorney general, I met with various Hawaiian sovereignty advocates about their continuing efforts and what positions I might take on behalf of the State. Consequently, I looked into the issue and kept an eye on it during my tenure, since the idea of federal recognition of a Hawaiian sovereign government had the potential to create lasting and substantial change for Hawai'i.

One important issue that has always come up in discussions of Hawaiian sovereignty is whether gambling would be prohibited. As noted earlier, gambling is a particularly sensitive issue in Hawai'i, which is politically liberal but socially conservative. As anti-gambling forces have had a strong presence and influence in Hawai'i over the years, they were attuned to the possibility that enacting some form of a Native Hawaiian government entity might result in the immediate legalization of gambling.

The federal courts in many decisions over many years have upheld the sovereign rights of Native American tribal governments and allowed them to conduct gambling on lands in "Indian country." The rise of gambling in numerous Indian jurisdictions, despite the prohibitions on gambling in surrounding states and counties, has been an unwelcome but unstoppable development for many states. Some have commented that gambling, with the host of social problems of addiction and profligate behavior that it brings, is the "revenge" of Native Americans on the white man.

Why raise an issue that will give rise to strong public opposition, especially where strong public support would be needed to create a Hawaiian government entity? A better political strategy is to seek allies instead of enemies. Consequently, as far as I can remember, all versions of the Akaka Bill have always prohibited gambling. However, this orthodoxy has been challenged in recent years, as the need for money to fund Native Hawaiian issues has become increasingly acute, and the lure of obtaining such money from gambling has become increasingly attractive.

The issues around Hawaiian sovereignty raised many interesting and fundamental questions about government and the State. How would creation and federal recognition of a Hawaiian government, of any form, affect the State? Whose laws would apply and where? Could state police follow criminals onto Hawaiian government lands and make arrests? Would Hawai'i criminal statutes apply to conduct on Hawaiian government lands? Would county building codes apply to construction on Hawaiian government lands? These are not trivial questions, as they go right to the heart of thousands of details of governing.

There is a significantly large body of law, much of it from the United States Supreme Court and other federal courts, which has arisen regarding "Indian" or Native American legal issues. Attorneys general from other states must deal with Indian law and jurisdictional issues. If a Hawaiian government were to receive federal recognition, would all of this Indian law immediately apply to the activities of that government? Would federal Indian law outweigh and be given more force and effect than Hawai'i state law and practice?

During my term, the issue did not come up in Congress, so we did not have to take a position. I tended to agree with the stance previously taken by Attorney General Bennett, that to protect the State, negotiations and agreement between the State and any Hawaiian government should be a precondition to federal recognition. But the opportunity did not arise for me to opine. Recognizing that the issue was unlikely to be successfully brought before Congress, President Barack Obama put into place a regulatory change at the Department of the Interior near the end of his term, providing for an administrative regulatory path to federal recognition of a Hawaiian governmental entity. However, to date, no consensus has been reached in the Hawaiian community to trigger such a process.

The opportunity to deal with Hawaiian legal issues, with all their complexity, history and political and cultural significance, was both gratifying and thought provoking. As a lawyer, the legal issues were fascinating, cutting-edge and unique, with scant precedent and no simple or easy solutions. As a decision maker, the legal and political issues were sobering because of their importance to the State and the people of Hawai'i, both Hawaiians and non-Hawaiians. There were aspects of social justice, constitutional dimensions, politics and culture, as well as fundamental governing issues that required consideration. I was pleased to have a seat at the table to make a contribution, no matter how modest, to the process of dealing with these issues.

The issues of how Hawai'i will deal with social problems that affect the Hawaiian community and the legacy of historical wrongs are similar in many ways to the issues of racial and social justice, which the United States must confront and deal with regarding Black, Latino, Asian American and Native American communities on the mainland. Although issues relating to Native Hawaiians are unique and distinct to Hawai'i, how Hawai'i deals with these issues of social justice will say a lot about the people of Hawai'i and the state's political leaders. Similarly, how America deals with the historical scars of slavery, genocide and other ills wrought upon people of color will say a lot about who Americans are as a people today, what we value, and whether we indeed adhere to the principles of the Constitution and the ideals of equality and justice for all. Whether legal and political solutions can be found that will, in some measure, provide a basis for addressing past wrongs and laying a foundation for the future, only time will tell. ❦

| 9 |

Crime and Punishment

James "Jimmy" Pflueger was one of Hawai'i's wealthiest people. He owned an auto dealership and along with his cousins had inherited thousands of acres of land on the islands of O'ahu and Kaua'i. In 2006, Ka Loko Dam, an old earthen dam on his property, overtopped and failed during heavy rainstorms. Pflueger had allegedly conducted grading operations near the dam without a permit, filling in the emergency spillway, which caused the dam's failure. The ensuing flash flood of 400 million gallons swept away numerous downstream houses in one of the worst disasters in Hawai'i history. Seven people tragically died as a result. Numerous civil suits were filed, but no criminal charges were brought on Kaua'i. It was widely believed that Pflueger regarded himself as above the law and had made illegal cash contributions to Kaua'i mayor Maryann Kusaka.

In 2008, my predecessor, Attorney General Mark Bennett, indicted Pflueger for manslaughter for his role in the deaths of these people. It was unusual for the attorney general to bring a criminal indictment for manslaughter, as such matters were normally handled by the prosecuting attorneys for the counties. But the Kaua'i County prosecuting attorney had failed to act in this case, and something needed to be done. The criminal prosecution was delayed for many years by various legal maneuvers by Pflueger while the civil suits were resolved. The case was still pending when I took office, so resolution fell to me.

As the case was coming up for trial, we evaluated the case and decided that in light of a lengthy trial, probable appeals and Pflueger's age, we could get a quicker resolution by a plea deal. Negotiations ensued for Pflueger's company, Pacific 808 Properties, to take responsibility for the seven counts of manslaughter and pay fines of $350,000, while Pflueger would plead no contest to a lesser charge of felony reckless endangerment and be sentenced. Pflueger accepted the proposed plea deal. At the sentencing hearing, the State recommended a sentence of one year of imprisonment and five years of probation for Pflueger. Judge Randall Valenciano noted that Pflueger appeared to believe he was above the law but was the person with ultimate responsibility. He sentenced Pflueger to jail time of seven months and five years of probation, but he reduced the fines against Pacific 808 Properties to $1,000 per count, as he apparently felt that Pflueger, rather than the company, should bear the punishment.

Strange as it may seem, the prosecution of Jimmy Pflueger was one of the few times I personally was involved as attorney general in the actual prosecution of a criminal case. While the attorney general is the chief law enforcement officer for the State, and enforcement of the criminal laws in Hawaiʻi is carried out under the attorney general's authority, most of the day-to-day prosecution of criminal matters in Hawaiʻi has long been delegated to the prosecuting attorneys for the counties, as political subdivisions of the State.

The prosecuting attorneys, rather than the attorney general, are dedicated to the prosecution of criminal matters and have large staffs to handle the nitty-gritty of criminal prosecutions on behalf of the State. While you might think that being the chief law enforcement officer, the top cop, meant that I spent most of my time putting bad guys behind bars, you would be wrong, because the prosecuting attorneys handle those duties. Instead, 95% of my time was spent dealing with civil laws, not criminal laws.

Nonetheless, the attorney general in Hawaiʻi still has significant law enforcement responsibilities. The attorney general has a Criminal Justice Division with a number of prosecuting attorneys who handle state crimes; crimes occurring on state property such as the airports or ʻIolani Palace; where prosecuting attorneys have conflicts such as prosecuting a county official, Medicaid fraud, embezzlement of state monies; or in limited cases where the attorney general decides to exercise authority, such as the prosecution of James Pflueger. However, these cases are few as compared to the normal workload of the prosecuting attorneys. The attorney general has the power to handle any prosecution and theoretically can take any given case away from a county prosecutor and prosecute it. However, that is generally not a practical solution and would work against the normal delegation of authority and the overarching goal of having law enforcement work together.

The attorney general also provides criminal justice resources for the community. The attorney general maintains the Internet Crimes Against Children (ICAC) office that sets up sting operations to take down child pornographers and pedophiles; the Crime Prevention and Justice Assistance Division (CPJAD) that provides research, technology and information resources to law enforcement; and the Hawai'i Criminal Justice Data Center (HCJDC) that provides real-time access to criminal history data for law enforcement. Additionally, the Investigation Division employed about fifty retired police officers who served both as investigators and as law enforcement officers when the need arose.

During my tenure, we arrested some pornographers and pedophiles and created a mobile phone app that provided information to the public about the addresses of convicted sex offenders. We investigated sex trafficking, since the issue of the forced trafficking of young girls has been a nationwide problem. However, very few arrests were being made in Hawai'i at that time, as sex trafficking had moved online and off of the Waikīkī streets. The business community was not complaining about overt sexual solicitation as in years past, sex trafficking was more difficult to spot, and it seemed like the police departments were not making a lot of arrests that could be prosecuted. In hindsight, I wish we had been able to do more to combat and stop sex trafficking, which is a pernicious problem.

I previously had limited experience as a criminal attorney. Most of my career was spent as a civil litigation lawyer, fighting over money rather than years of a man's life. In law school I had spent a summer working for the federal public defender in San Francisco. I worked on cases defending criminals who didn't seem to watch TV or have much common sense. One was a bank robber who had taped some flares together to pretend they were dynamite and wired them to an alarm clock. He gave a bank teller a note demanding money or he would blow everyone up. The teller started laughing, and the robber was arrested by a guard and caught on five different cameras. I decided then that I wanted a better class of clientele than the criminal defendants I was seeing, so I gravitated to civil litigation. As a young lawyer I handled a few cases for the federal public defender in Honolulu on a contract basis to gain trial experience.

Still, an important part of the job as attorney general was working on various matters with people in law enforcement, and I took this responsibility seriously. It always seemed to me that a lot of criminal behavior arises from people acting out the seven deadly sins—pride, greed, lust, envy, gluttony, wrath and sloth. Criminal laws exist to protect the community and keep people safe from the effects of such bad behavior while punishing criminals to deter such acts.

As attorney general, I also got involved in a number of legal issues relating to the prisons, which are administered by the Department of Public Safety (DPS). There were many legal issues that arose relating to DPS and the prisons. How are prisoners to be accommodated in the exercise of their religious freedoms, both in conventional religions as well as Hawaiian cultural beliefs? Reasonable accommodation had to be provided. How was DPS improving its management policies and execution under the watchful eye of a federal monitor pursuant to a consent decree entered into to settle lawsuits against the State due to substantial overcrowding and a number of suicides? DPS had to take proactive steps to work with the federal monitor to improve conditions. Could prison parole policies be reformed to utilize newly developed evidence-based systems and models to allow more nonviolent offenders to be released, monitored and rehabilitated? Efforts at reforms were considered. Gov. Abercrombie was very interested in prison issues, especially investigations of pardon applications, as he had worked as a probation officer early in his career. We considered all of these issues and more.

The State has an incredible amount of resources and power to deter and punish criminal behavior, but it cannot abuse that power by using it arbitrarily or indiscriminately. The State has to use its power evenhandedly and with appropriate discretion. Because I did not have career experience as a prosecutor or criminal attorney, I had not spent much time developing a particular point of view on many law enforcement policy matters. However, since the State's resources regarding law enforcement were within my purview, I wanted to make sure that law enforcement was carried out reasonably and judiciously. A couple of law enforcement matters came up during my tenure that gave me some important insights.

Smoke 'em if You've Got 'em

One of the first things I did as attorney general was to convene a meeting of the Law Enforcement Coalition (LEC). The LEC consists of all of the prosecutors and police chiefs of the various counties—O'ahu, Kaua'i, Maui, Hawai'i—as well as with the US attorney, the FBI special agent in charge and the US marshal. The purpose of the LEC was to have the law enforcement community come together at least once a year, just prior to the legislative session, to discuss any legislative initiatives or issues that were coming up, coordinate our response and have the law enforcement community speak with one voice.

We met in the attorney general's conference room. Because I had not been a prosecutor or involved in criminal law matters, I was new to the group and an unknown quantity, but I was the attorney general, the nominal leader of the LEC. The first issue to arise was marijuana. The question that the prosecutors, police chiefs and federal law enforcement wanted to know was what was my position on marijuana?

Proponents of marijuana legalization had sought approval at the legislature for many years. Medical marijuana had been allowed in Hawai'i on a limited scale since 2000, over the objections of law enforcement. Every year, the pro-marijuana forces, lobbyists and monied interests tried to get further gains, an enlargement of medical marijuana provisions, or outright legalization of recreational marijuana, but they had not been successful. Every year, law enforcement had opposed such legalization. However, in 2011 there was a big push nationally to expand medical and even recreational marijuana, and it was anticipated that legislative bills to achieve those goals were coming.

The LEC group seemed wary of Gov. Abercrombie and me, the new attorney general, on this question. Many people thought that Gov. Abercrombie was an unrepentant hippie from the 1960s who would favor marijuana, and I was an unknown. Did I share their values and goals? Or would I abandon one of local law enforcement's strongest tenets? It was almost a litmus test.

I considered this question in light of my own experience. While I had criticized abuses by law enforcement, I still very much supported law enforcement and the critical role in our community of first responders and the thin blue line. I had smoked marijuana in college without bad effect, but I had given it up and was not an ideological proponent of legalization. The question I asked back was what is the basis for opposing legalization, decriminalization or the relaxation of medical marijuana restrictions?

The response from the most vocal proponents in the LEC group was unsatisfactory. "It is a gateway drug." Since the 1960s I had heard this shibboleth that marijuana would lead to hard drugs like cocaine and heroin, and I felt that it was probably not true. This appeared to be an article of faith among most of the LEC group, but it was too simplistic and rote for me to adopt. I asked the police chiefs and prosecutors what studies and research they had to support their position, since I had not looked at the issue for many years. They did not have much.

Still, the purpose of LEC was to have a unified law enforcement position, and it was clear that most of the group were against any further legalization of marijuana. I also thought that I would need to work with the law enforcement community on many issues during my term, and I was reluctant to break with them at the outset if it could be avoided. The attorney general had previously opposed legalization or further decriminalization of marijuana. So my response was that I would be happy to stand with them on this issue, but that I would be looking for more and better research and rationales on these issues to see whether we would change the position.

I then spoke to Gov. Abercrombie about this. His position was that it was not a major issue for him one way or the other, and that he really didn't "give a shit about a pothead in Puna." Puna is a district on the Big Island of Hawai'i known as a hotbed of marijuana cultivation and use. In other words, he would not be leading any charge for or against further legalization of marijuana and would leave it to the legislature.

Shortly after the LEC meeting, a marijuana legalization bill came up for hearing in the legislature. The attorney general follows many bills in the legislature, offering testimony where appropriate. Much of the time, the testimony concerns constitutional, administrative or procedural matters, i.e., does the legislation violate a constitutional provision, is it vague or ambiguous, does it contradict other laws? While many policy matters are left to the legislature, the attorney general does weigh in on policy relating to law enforcement. Various deputy attorneys general draft testimony to be presented to legislative committees, all of which was reviewed by me and Joshua Wisch, my special executive assistant, to make sure that the attorney general agrees with the legal and policy implications of such testimony.

In this context I reviewed some testimony prepared by one of the criminal justice deputies opposing a bill to decriminalize possession of an ounce of marijuana. The testimony argued that decriminalizing a single ounce of marijuana would be a grave mistake, because a single ounce of marijuana could produce sixty marijuana "joints," or cigarettes, thus making the possessor of an ounce of marijuana a potential drug dealer, in possession of far more than would be needed for a casual consumer.

This testimony struck me as odd and contradicted my personal experience as a college student in the early 1970s. Even the strongest marijuana at that time was not so potent or powerful as to be able to provide sixty cigarettes from a single ounce. This seemed to me to be an outlandish claim. I questioned the deputy attorney general who had written the testimony about the basis for this statement. He told me that there was ample research and background to justify the testimony.

Because of my stance on allowing the policy on marijuana to continue until I was satisfied it should be changed, I was still getting my footing as attorney general, and because the testimony was due that day, I decided to defer to the deputy. I checked with other criminal deputies who also said this was fact. Since the deputy would be the one testifying and I would not be appearing, I signed off on the testimony, with some misgivings. What I did not understand at the time was that all written testimony from the attorney general would bear my name and be "my" testimony, even if one of the deputies would be actually speaking to the legislative committee.

The next morning Civil Beat, a Hawai'i online investigative newspaper underwritten by eBay founder Pierre Omidyar, blared out the story: Attorney General David Louie testifies that an ounce of marijuana contains sixty joints—does he know what the heck he is talking about? Civil Beat said it was going to research this and confirm whether I knew what I was talking about or if I was just blowing smoke. Because of my own doubts about the veracity of this statement, which now was being attributed to me, I became concerned. I was a little worried that I might be exposed as a charlatan, trying to peddle facts that were untrue, in my first major news story about a law enforcement policy position.

I immediately called up the deputy who had drafted the testimony and asked what citation, research, study or publication we had to support this statement. His response caused me to have a moment of anxiety. "A cop on Maui told me this," he said. No, I said, I want the study or paper. "Nope, just a cop on Maui." No study, no research, no article. Just an article of faith, like marijuana is a gateway drug. This did not comfort me in the least. So I tasked Wisch to find something, anything, that would justify the position that we had taken. After a couple of hours of research he was unable to find anything. This definitely did not ease my concerns.

The next morning Civil Beat reported that although sixty joints to an ounce seemed like an awful lot, marijuana these days is so potent and powerful that *High Times*, the most prominent marijuana industry magazine, and the National Organization for the Reform of Marijuana Laws (NORML), the lobbying organization promoting the legalization of marijuana, both reported that a person could actually get eighty marijuana cigarettes or joints out of an ounce of really good marijuana, so my testimony fell well within the range of possible. Whew!

What did I learn from this little episode? I learned to make darn sure that I was comfortable with any testimony that went out. After that I reviewed all draft testimony very carefully, since it was all going out under my name. And I decided not to defer to anyone on something I questioned without drilling down and satisfying myself as to the ultimate conclusion. You would think I would have learned all of that after thirty years of practice as an attorney. However, because I was new to the position, unfamiliar with the procedures and in a hurry, I had deferred to someone who turned out to be taking something on faith, rather than rational analysis. It was a valuable lesson to learn all over again.

Subsequently, I did satisfy myself that there was sufficient research and analytical studies that showed that marijuana is bad for young people, that it can hamper and impair their mental development, that legalization or decriminalization increases the risks that young people will use marijuana, and that it is not good for our communities to have more impaired people, especially if they are driving. The studies were enough to convince me that marijuana, while certainly not necessarily a gateway drug to heroin or cocaine or harder drugs, was still not a good thing for our youth and communities. I thus continued the position of the attorney general's office through my tenure against legalization or decriminalization of marijuana. Since that time, however, numerous states have legalized recreational marijuana, and Hawai'i has expanded the use of medical marijuana by legalizing dispensaries.

Moreover, as shown by the local and national developments on marijuana just in the past few years, what constitutes appropriate boundaries for criminalized behavior is a constantly evolving process as societal mores change. In the 1920s, Prohibition made the manufacture, sale and consumption of alcohol illegal. Yet that all changed, and alcohol again became widely accepted. Similarly, medical and recreational marijuana now appear to be headed for widespread acceptance, despite the misgivings of law enforcement leaders who still think that it is a gateway drug that only leads to the breakdown of society.

Moloka'i—The Friendly Isle

Moloka'i is nicknamed "The Friendly Island." It is the most undeveloped of the major islands and has beautiful pristine beaches, soaring cliffs and breathtakingly lovely views. Moloka'i has a rich tradition of Native Hawaiian cultural traditions and friendly people, but it is off the beaten tourist track and its economy has been mostly based on agriculture and subsistence, rather than tourism. The tourism that has developed has emphasized outdoor pursuits such as fishing, hunting and hiking. No major hotel developments have been successful on Moloka'i. The local community had been active for decades to inhibit and prevent development, seeming to prefer a slower and more rural lifestyle compared to urban Honolulu and Waikīkī.

In the fall of 2011, there were some decidedly *unfriendly* incidents on Moloka'i that precipitated a possible law enforcement response. American Safari Cruises, a small cruise ship company, announced that it would be bringing ships to dock in Moloka'i's harbor. When the *Safari Explorer*, a small ship with eighteen staterooms, arrived, it was blocked from docking on two occasions by a handful of activists on surfboards and small boats. The company had contracts and permits to make regular stops at Moloka'i, as a different type of tourist experience. The company reached out to the governor's office and asked for assistance. That's when I got involved.

Protests against ships docking in harbors had a history on Kaua'i and Moloka'i. In 2007, a floating blockade of surfers, canoes, small boats and jet skis prevented the Hawai'i Superferry, a gigantic catamaran ferry, from docking at Kaua'i's Nāwiliwili Harbor. The Superferry's operators sought to develop an interisland ferry system with two mega-ships that could quickly transport cars and people back and forth between O'ahu, Maui and Kaua'i within hours, rivaling the use of planes. Although it had support from Gov. Linda Lingle and the legislature, it became a flashpoint and poster child for antidevelopment forces. Court challenges resulted in two rulings by the Hawai'i Supreme Court that prohibited Superferry operations without a prohibitively massive, expensive and time-consuming environmental impact statement (EIS). Such an EIS was never pursued, and the Superferry project died.

With that history, what was government supposed to do about these protests on Moloka'i? The protestors had a right to protest. They were against development, cruise ships and things they felt would change their way of life. Some people said the cruise company had not given the community sufficient notice. But the cruise ship company had proper permits to dock and conduct operations. They were not required by law to give additional notice or to make donations to community organizations that might buy peace. The State had an obligation to protect the company's right to operate.

Nonetheless, it was clear that some people on Moloka'i were angry and upset about this and would not hesitate to jump in the water on their surfboards and canoes to physically obstruct the docking of the ship. Since the cruise ship was planning to come back in another two weeks, we had a short period of time to figure out what to do.

Fortunately, we had some experience in this area. A few months earlier the Office of the Attorney General had been involved in planning for protests in waterfront and beach areas in Waikīkī in connection with the Asia-Pacific Economic Cooperation (APEC) Economic Leaders' Meeting. President Barack Obama hosted the leaders of nine APEC nations who gathered to negotiate the Trans-Pacific Strategic Economic Partnership multilateral free trade agreement. It was the largest international conference ever staged in Hawai'i.

When the World Trade Organization held a similar conference in Seattle in 1999, there had been extensive and disruptive protests and even riots. Hawai'i was concerned that similar protests might occur at the APEC meeting, resulting in active planning to deal with protests as well as to provide security against possible attacks on the world leaders who were planning to attend. This included planning for protests in the water and on the beaches in Waikīkī, so we coordinated with the Coast Guard. The APEC meeting went off without a hitch. That experience was invaluable and helped us to plan for the anticipated protests on Moloka'i.

The Moloka'i protests were a major challenge to the authority of the State and law enforcement. Gov. Abercrombie was adamant that the protestors, no matter how well intentioned, should not be allowed to obstruct lawful commerce and shipping. Our mission was to figure out a way to stand up and execute a law enforcement operation, if necessary, to arrest protestors and clear the waters so that the cruise ship could dock.

One major problem was logistics. Moloka'i is relatively remote, with very limited police facilities. As part of the County of Maui, police presence was normally provided by two officers who would come each day from Maui. There was a very small jail, but no court or holding facilities that could be used to process large numbers of people who might be arrested. The harbor and water were a federal jurisdiction, governed by the Coast Guard, but there were no federal law enforcement presence or facilities on Moloka'i. We had to figure out how we were going to make arrests, get protestors out of the water who might actively and violently resist arrest, and process any arrestees. We planned for Coast Guard personnel, Maui police officers, State Harbors officers, State Division of Forestry and Wildlife (DOFAW) officers and investigators (retired police officers) from the Department of the Attorney General to be present, along with jet skis and boats, so that arrests could be made. We planned to set up tents to process arrestees and then transport them to Maui for booking.

Our ace in the hole was the threat that because the harbor and the waters involved federal jurisdiction, any arrestee would face federal prosecution that carried significant penalties, much greater than any state penalties. The state penalty for obstruction of vehicles was a petty misdemeanor with a very small fine. In other words, the applicable state laws were almost a toothless paper tiger. However, the violation of federal law involved the possibility of six months of jail time and having a permanent criminal record, which could have severe consequences for future travel and job opportunities.

Once we completed our planning, we asked William Aila, a prominent Native Hawaiian leader who was chairperson of the Board of Land and Natural Resources (BLNR) and executive head of the Department of Land and Natural Resources (DLNR), to negotiate with community leaders on Moloka'i to see if he could defuse the situation. He went and explained the hammer of federal prosecution, the significant downside risk that protestors would encounter and the State's willingness to make arrests, if necessary.

Aila's negotiations were successful. He convinced the Moloka'i community leaders, activists and protestors to stand down. They did not get into the water or block the cruise ship from docking. Of course, there were still some lingering problems, but not about docking. A few people cut down trees to block roads and vehicles transporting cruise ship passengers to visit points of interest. About a year later, the cruise ship company negotiated an agreement with the Moloka'i community on how to conduct the tours, including arrangements to use some tour businesses owned by Moloka'i residents.

What did I learn from this Moloka'i episode? This was a significant challenge to the State's authority. In my view it had to be met with planning for the use of substantial and possibly overwhelming force, and then negotiations to try to defuse the situation. It was unclear how many protestors might get into the water, but we had to be ready to arrest dozens of protestors, and possibly more. While I respected the point of view of the protestors, it was my duty as chief law enforcement officer to uphold the rights of the cruise ship company. Fortunately, the threat of federal criminal prosecution with significant penalties was a big enough deterrent to get protestors to stand down.

This Moloka'i episode was one of a number of antidevelopment, anti-growth protests that have occurred in the Islands over the past forty years. The Superferry protests were some of the bigger ones, but there have been several others. Recently, and subsequent to my tenure as attorney general, there have been continuing huge protests against the development of the Thirty Meter Telescope (TMT) on Mauna Kea on the Big Island. Thousands of protestors have gone up to Mauna Kea, some camping and staying for weeks and months on end, to block the access road to the top of the 13,800-foot mountain and prevent construction of a state-of-the-art telescope by an international consortium of universities and science benefactors. The protestors call themselves the *kia'i*, the "protectors," and say that Mauna Kea is sacred ground that has been desecrated by the mountain's earlier telescopes. The protests have been a rallying cry and flashpoint for Hawaiian issues, sovereignty and grievances. It is clear that the protests seek to address matters far beyond the construction of TMT. Surveys have shown significant support for the protestors, but even larger support for TMT.

Some have suggested using an overwhelming law enforcement presence to clear the access road and allow construction to proceed. Others have cautioned against mass arrests of Native Hawaiians and *kūpuna* (elders). Initially, Gov. David Ige called out a large police presence, issued an emergency proclamation and considered activating the National Guard, though he did not do so. For now, there is impasse and a standoff, while some negotiations and communications continue.

Upholding the rule of law is a singularly important and guiding principle for the attorney general, but sometimes there are factors that need to be addressed and considered by political leaders and other decision makers. Hopefully, this issue will be solved in a manner that respects Hawaiian culture and also respects the rights of the TMT project and the management of Mauna Kea, in a way that heals divisions rather than creates more of them. It is a difficult problem to solve.

In a general sense, law enforcement is one of the most important aspects of the job of the attorney general. My involvement in all of these issues led me to think about the many competing and complex considerations involved in law enforcement. As chief law enforcement officer, the attorney general is a proponent, spokesperson and symbol. Making sure that criminal laws are upheld and enforced, making sure that criminal law policies are rational and evenhanded, and keeping the public safe and secure from criminal behavior are all critical functions of government. Because most people are law-abiding citizens, the actual number of criminals is not large and most day-to-day prosecutions have been delegated to the county prosecutors, the time spent by me in dealing with criminal issues was a relatively small part of the job of Hawai'i's attorney general. However, the issues were interesting and important, as they often involved analysis of constitutional dimensions and legal principles, since freedom and rights were involved. For me it was an unparalleled view of how government works to keep our communities safe.

| 10 |

Preserving the ʻĀina

In the 1970s, singer Joni Mitchell wrote and recorded the popular song "Big Yellow Taxi," partly about the pink Royal Hawaiian Hotel in Waikīkī, lamenting that, "They paved paradise and put up a parking lot." When I moved to Hawai'i I experienced the pristine white sandy beaches and azure blue waters, hiked the otherworldly volcanic crater of Haleakalā and took note of the rare plants and birds. These experiences reinforced and deepened my appreciation for the special blessings of our natural environment. Perhaps because Hawai'i is such an incredible paradise, people here are very conscious of being stewards of the land and have engaged in many legal and political protests over the years to preserve the environment from development and other threats.

As attorney general I had the opportunity to consider a number of environmental legal issues. I thought it was important to protect the environment and the *ʻāina* (the land) for future generations. My office was charged with enforcing Hawai'i's environmental laws and working closely with the US Environmental Protection Agency (EPA) to enforce federal laws. Hawai'i's constitution reinforces the importance of the environment as it states, "Each person has the right to a clean and healthful environment." Numerous State agencies have responsibilities regarding the environment, including the Department of Health (DOH) that regulates pollution, the Department of Land and Natural Resources (DLNR) that manages State lands, the Commission on Water Resource Management that manages the critical resource of fresh water, and a specialized Environmental Court, only the second such court in the nation.

For the Birds

Interestingly, one of the first environmental matters to cross my desk as attorney general was not to enforce such laws against others, but instead to defend the State from a claim that Hawaiʻi was violating federal environmental laws, along with a threat by a junior US attorney to criminally prosecute the State in this regard.

Newell's shearwaters are seagoing birds that fly and nest in and around Hawaiʻi, and their last major breeding colonies are on Kauaʻi. The name comes from their habit of gliding along the troughs of waves, seeming to "shear" off the tips of the waves. Because of dwindling numbers, shearwaters are classified as an endangered species and protected by the Migratory Bird Treaty Act (MBTA), which is administered by the US Fish & Wildlife Service (USFW). Shearwaters use the moon to fly at night and can get disoriented by bright stadium and highway lights, which cause them to fly around and around until they get exhausted and fall to the ground, becoming roadkill or prey for cats and dogs.

In 2010, the USFW forced the County of Kauaʻi and the Kauaʻi Island Utility Cooperative (KIUC) to shut down all high school night football games because the bright stadium lights were causing harm to the shearwaters, especially during their breeding season. On a small island like Kauaʻi, night football games were a major community event. But it's hard to argue with the federal government, so the county and KIUC agreed to the shutdown.

In 2012, a young US attorney in Washington, DC, thought he would make his reputation by threatening the Hawaiʻi Department of Transportation (DOT) with criminal prosecution for allegedly failing to more quickly retrofit and change out all highway lights across the state to protect shearwaters. It was simultaneously audacious and obnoxious as a legal ploy, but it certainly got my attention.

DOT had been in discussions with USFW for years and was already proceeding with a retrofit program. USFW wanted the retrofitting to go faster. While protection of the shearwaters was important, a quicker retrofit of all highway lights in the state would cost a lot more money and still take time. When he and I would discuss various national challenges, my friend Dustin McDaniel, the attorney general of Arkansas, used to say, "All it takes is money." Unfortunately, in Hawaiʻi state government in 2012, money was in short supply. Besides, the DOT had already committed its funding to many other essential infrastructure projects.

The US attorney representing USFW wanted to force DOT to move the retrofit program to the top of the list, using the threat of criminal prosecution as a cudgel. Since USFW had been successful in shutting down the Friday night football lights on Kaua'i, they thought a similar heavy-handed approach would work with the State. Not so fast. Our legal research showed that there was no precedent for the federal government to criminally prosecute the State. Although we were right, proving our position would likely require us to fight this novel approach in court.

There was another way. The attorney general is a member of the National Association of Attorneys General (NAAG), a group composed of all the states and territories of the United States. NAAG had two meetings a year that provided a forum for interacting with fellow attorneys general to discuss issues of mutual interest. The annual meeting in Washington, DC, was coming up, and Attorney General Eric Holder was scheduled to speak to us. This was a perfect opportunity to escalate this off-the-wall threat to the top of the food chain.

At the NAAG meeting, Attorney General Holder, whom I had met previously, gave a great speech, took questions and then walked around the room to talk with each of the attorneys general. I took the opportunity to tell him that one of his low-level assistant US attorneys was trying to declare the State of Hawai'i (the government of President Obama's birthplace) to be a criminal enterprise, and that we did not think that was appropriate. Tony West, who was the associate attorney general, the next highest ranking official in the Department of Justice, was with Attorney General Holder and said he would look into this and get back to me.

A week later I got a call from the Department of Justice supervisor in charge of USFW matters. I said we were happy to negotiate, but that it was absolutely unacceptable for a US attorney to threaten the State with criminal prosecution. We then had several phone conversations with her and her team about the issues. They wanted to move the retrofit timetable up, and we wanted to keep it the same.

It's funny how sometimes decisions on important issues can turn on small interpersonal dynamics. On all of the calls, I always asked everyone to identify themselves. The low-level US attorney who had started the whole thing was not identified on any of these calls. But then he called me to negotiate a point and let slip that he knew what was going on because he had been listening in on the previous calls. Amazing. I immediately called up the supervisor, told her about this admission and said it was obvious that she and her attorneys had been lying to me. I told her I was no longer willing to trust anything she or her team might say, and that I intended to escalate this up to Attorney General Holder.

The dynamic changed. A few days later I got a call from the supervisor. They agreed to drop the matter and the idea of filing criminal proceedings against Hawaiʻi. She also said that the low-level US attorney was no longer involved. Goal accomplished. The DOT still had to proceed forward with its highway lights retrofit project, but the pressure to have that project become priority number one disappeared.

Environmental Activism in Hawaiʻi

Even before the 1960s, when Rachel Carson wrote *Silent Spring* and gave rise to a national environmental movement, people in Hawaiʻi had been actively concerned about preserving their paradise. There have been many grassroots organizations in Hawaiʻi dedicated to protecting the environment against development. Life of the Land, the Sierra Club and Save Our Surf are just some of the local organizations that have been involved in political efforts as well as litigation. The Save Sandy Beach/ Ka Iwi Coalition in the 1980s prevented the development of thirty acres of one of the last open and wild coastlines on Oʻahu by Kamehameha Schools/Bishop Estate, the largest, most politically connected and most powerful landowner in Hawaiʻi.

At times, environmental concerns have overlapped and blended with Hawaiian issues, as broad coalitions were formed to stop development or other harmful activities and preserve the land. In the 1970s and 1980s, a broad movement arose to stop the US Navy from continuing to use the uninhabited island of Kahoʻolawe as a bombing target. When I first came to Hawaiʻi in 1976 as a law clerk, I watched the court proceedings in US district court over the arrests of Native Hawaiian activists who had occupied Kahoʻolawe to protest the bombings. National security concerns were cited by the Navy to justify the bombings, but eventually those gave way to the environmental and Hawaiian concerns. The bombing was curtailed, and a plan was set in motion to reclaim areas of the island and remove unexploded ordnance.

At other times, environmental concerns have been adverse to Hawaiian issues. I remember being involved where USFW sought to block a planned housing development by DHHL on the Big Island. USFW had determined that there was an endangered moss species that only grew in a few places, and that one of those places was where DHHL wanted to build houses. The problem was made more complicated by the position of USFW that DHHL could not build in certain areas that were favorable habitat areas for the moss, even though no moss yet existed in those areas. Because USFW was a federal agency, enforcing federal laws, it could override the mandate of DHHL. Negotiations over what development might be allowed, and under what circumstances, were still proceeding when I left office.

There is never a shortage of legal matters relating to the environment in Hawai'i, and I was regularly briefed about ongoing enforcement efforts. Being involved with such efforts always felt very satisfying. Various deputy attorneys general worked with the DOH to enforce environmental laws relating to the discharge of sewage treatment and outfall pipes of the City & County of Honolulu and the County of Maui. During my tenure there were ongoing efforts to curtail the use of cesspools and upgrade sewage treatment in rural areas. After I left office, a recent US Supreme Court case, *County of Maui v. Hawai'i Wildlife Fund*, ruled that the county could not continue to allow sewage wastewater to be discharged into the ground in coastline areas, as the effluent seeped through the ground to pollute the ocean in violation of the Clean Water Act. Another major ongoing environmental concern in Hawai'i I followed was the past and possibly future fuel leakage by a dozen gigantic metal fuel storage tanks owned by the US Navy, which threatens to contaminate Honolulu's main aquifer for fresh drinking water. For years, the Navy has been reluctant to follow existing EPA guidelines, such as adding double wall protection (creating a tank within a tank). Unfortunately, Hawai'i has so far been unable to force Navy compliance, but efforts have continued, and the Navy recently made a proposal to implement double wall protection.

Turtle Bay

Turtle Bay is on the legendary North Shore of the island of O'ahu. It is named after the large number of green sea turtles who live in the area and used to lay their eggs at the bay. Almost 850 acres owned by a developer is still mostly undeveloped and features beautiful beaches, a scenic rugged shoreline, hiking trails, horse stables and trails and two golf courses designed by Arnold Palmer set next to a hotel and a number of condominiums. The area also included Kawela Bay, a beautiful, secluded bay with a sheltered palm tree-lined beach, where swimming, boating, stand-up paddling and kayaking could occur without the rough waters and pounding waves of the rest of the coastline.

I worked with others to establish a conservation easement on 665 acres of land at Turtle Bay that was otherwise slated for a massive development. By obtaining agreement and securing $40 million of state funding for the conservation easement, we were able to restrict future development on much of the area, including an undeveloped shoreline of Kawela Bay, and preserve it all in a natural state for future generations to enjoy. Here's how it happened.

To put things into historical context, the Turtle Bay Resort opened in 1972 with approximately 450 hotel rooms, along with some nearby condominium units. Various developers periodically sought to build more hotels and condominiums. In the mid-1980s, the then-owner, Kuilima Development Company (KDC), obtained entitlements (government approvals) from the City & County of Honolulu (City) for an expansion of 4,000 units. KDC submitted an environmental impact statement (EIS) in 1985 to justify this expansion, but never proceeded with construction.

In 2005, Oaktree Capital Management, a new developer who bought the property, sought to dust off the entitlements and build five new hotels with an additional 3,500 rooms and condominiums. Times had changed, and these plans alarmed the rural North Shore community. Concerned about overcrowding and a dramatic change to the community character, community groups opposing development organized under the slogan "Keep the Country Country!" A lawsuit was filed to stop the development on the grounds that although no time deadlines existed for the entitlements, the old EIS had essentially expired and could no longer be used. In 2010 the Hawaiʻi Supreme Court agreed, holding that twenty-five years was too long a period for using the old entitlements, since the surrounding area had changed, and required the developer to provide a supplemental EIS (SEIS).

A new SEIS prepared in 2013 again proposed a full buildout of an additional 3,500 rooms and housing units, but it also proposed some reduced density alternatives for either 1,375 rooms and units, or 500 residential units only. The development plans proposed placing a number of luxury homes at Kawela Bay. Community groups again organized against further development, and three new lawsuits were filed to challenge the development.

On a parallel track, for several years the Hawaiʻi chapter of the Trust for Public Land, led by Lea Hong, along with the Nature Conservancy, had been negotiating with the developer to buy a conservation easement to preserve some of the Turtle Bay land in the area. A conservation easement is a contractual pledge by a landowner that prohibits further development of a particular parcel of land. Because this restriction goes on the title, it prevents any further development in perpetuity. Because the landowner gives up all development rights, a conservation easement may cost 80% to 90% of the full value of the land.

Part of Gov. Abercrombie's vision for O'ahu was that development to provide critical housing should be concentrated in the urban core of Honolulu. Antidevelopment activists are sometimes opposed to any development anywhere, but as the population grows and there is demand for housing, there is pressure to build. The conundrum of development for an island community is where do you allow development to fill the needs? Gov. Abercrombie was already working with the Hawai'i Community Development Authority (HCDA) to fast-track high-rise development in the Kaka'ako Mauka area next to downtown Honolulu.

At the beginning of the 2014 legislative session, Gov. Abercrombie announced that he wanted to solve the long-standing problems at Turtle Bay by allocating $40 million in State bond monies to buy a conservation easement. The bonding capacity for the State is a financial tool that allows the State to borrow money at favorable interest rates, as the State is generally regarded as a good credit risk. This bonding capacity is usually used to finance construction projects. The legislature usually self imposes an artificial bonding capacity cap each year, so that it does not engage in excessive borrowing, as the bonds have to be paid with general tax revenues. As the session proceeded, negotiations were ongoing with the Turtle Bay developer, but no deal was imminent, and Gov. Abercrombie's $40 million proposal had competition from other bonding capacity pet projects of legislators.

This is where I parachuted into the picture. The 2014 legislative session was more than halfway over when I got a call from the governor's office. Could I come in, with approximately one month left on the legislative calendar, to help close a deal with the Turtle Bay developer and get legislative funding? Of course. I met with Blake Oshiro, the governor's deputy chief of staff, and Julie China, one of the deputy attorneys general, to find out where we stood. China had been working with Paul Cool, an appraiser, and had been negotiating with Drew Stotesbury, the representative for Turtle Bay's owner. They had not reached a deal and were not close.

The State wanted a conservation easement on all of the remaining undeveloped lands at Turtle Bay. Because Gov. Abercrombie had already announced his intention to ask the legislature for $40 million, we were playing with our cards face up. Cool had appraised the value of a conservation easement for the remaining lands at around $35 million. Unfortunately, Turtle Bay had a different appraiser who valued its lands at approximately $60 million. The parties were at an impasse.

If we were going to do a deal, we had to quickly get agreement with Turtle Bay, then get legislative funding for $40 million. The time to get legislative funding was slipping away. There were several other factors that might add to and help cement a deal, but we still had to get a basic agreement for the State. Turtle Bay had long ago committed to the City that it would set aside about five acres of land near Kawela Bay for a park, and the City also had some funds that it could contribute to help purchase a conservation easement. The Trust for Public Land and the Nature Conservancy were also willing to raise and contribute additional funds.

China, Cool and I rolled up our sleeves, sat down with the dueling appraisal reports, maps and plans for the developments and tried to figure out how we could make a deal. The developer wanted full development but was willing to consider a conservation easement. Normally, for a developer to realize a profit, it has to actually develop a project, build it out and sell it. Such a process can take years and requires substantial capital. On the other hand, the sale of a conservation easement can put money in the developer's pocket immediately, without any of the risks of planning, financing, building and selling.

Many hotel development interests are owned by entities that are interested in realizing and maximizing profits, and Turtle Bay was no different. The Turtle Bay developer had already been stymied by the adverse rulings of the Hawaiʻi Supreme Court, the continued protests of the North Shore community and the prospect of further lawsuits. A conservation easement was a viable way to extract significant money from the land, avoid contentious and time-consuming litigation and move onto something else.

It was apparent that the parties were too far apart on their appraisal values to reach a deal for a conservation easement on the entire property. We had no more than $40 million of State money to spend (which they knew), and it was unlikely that Turtle Bay would shave one-third off their stated price. Although we thought we could get an additional $5 million from the City and $3.5 million from the Nature Conservancy and the Trust for Public Land, the most we could raise would be about $48.5 million. How could we negotiate the various component parts of the property to get the best conservation easement for the money?

Kawela Bay was clearly the crown jewel and was the most expensive of the parts. Because it was a pristine bay with lovely views, Turtle Bay could command premium prices for house lots there. Other coastline areas would also have views, but without a bay they would not be as desirable or pricey. From the State's perspective, it was most important to stop development at Kawela Bay and any coastline areas, if we could afford it. The presence of homes in those locations would stifle public access. Residential lots on the interior of the property away from the ocean did not appear as valuable, although Turtle Bay valued them at high prices. I was willing to let those go, since I did not believe they would really be developed. Finally, it was very important for the State and conservation groups to preserve public access to the shoreline and existing hiking trails in and around the Turtle Bay property.

I had a few meetings and phone calls with Stotesbury to exchange offers. We both knew that time was short, and we had to cut to the chase. Stotesbury negotiated hard but also demonstrated flexibility. After a few exchanges, we reached a deal. For $40 million we would get a conservation easement over a large portion of the property, including Kawela Bay and the coastline areas, while leaving out some areas for future development of another hotel and some condominiums. We built in some contingencies around the use of additional monies being provided by the City, the Nature Conservancy and the Trust for Public Land.

Of course, reaching a deal with Turtle Bay was only half the equation. The remaining challenge was to secure legislative funding. This was not an easy task, as we were near the end of the session, we needed various committee approvals, and the money chairs, Representative Sylvia Luke for the House Finance Committee and Senator David Ige (now Hawai'i's governor) for the Senate Ways and Means Committee, had not committed to the requested funding. It was unclear whether there was room in the self-imposed legislative bonding authority cap. While the cap could be exceeded if the legislators wanted, it was *their* cap, not ours, so it was unlikely they would do so just because the governor asked.

As we put together a strategy to get legislative approval, I began working with Senator Clayton Hee, as well as Lea Hong, Denise Antolini and others in the environmental community, to lobby the legislature.

They say politics makes strange bedfellows. Hee had been my nemesis during my confirmation a few years earlier. Over time I had developed a working relationship with him, as he was the Senate judiciary chair, I appeared in front of him for hearings on many matters, and he was friends with the governor. He wanted to preserve the North Shore, which was part of the district he represented, and had previously been involved in numerous environmental causes. We were allies on this matter, and Hee employed his talents to help secure funding for the conservation easement and get the measure passed in the Senate.

The House was another matter, as there appeared to be more resistance than in the Senate. Oshiro and the governor's legislative team, along with environmental activists, worked the halls as we met with several House committees and the Democratic Caucus to sell the deal to the House. As we came down to the wire, it appeared that we had approval from all necessary corners except for the money chairs. We also understood that both the Senate and House had already allocated the full amount of the cap of the State's bonding capacity, which they were not going to raise.

It was time for some creative financing. Kalbert Young, the budget and finance director, got involved to find a way to fund the State's $40 million share. Normally, bonding was obtained through general obligation bonds that would be paid off by general tax dollars, and the legislative cap applied to such bonds. But the cap did not apply if another state agency issued the bonds and found a way to pay for them. Young proposed to have the Hawaiʻi Tourism Authority (HTA) issue revenue bonds and pay for them using its share of transient accommodation (hotel) taxes. Keeping the beauty of the land in a natural undeveloped state is an important part of tourism, so there was a clear public purpose involved in using HTA. I didn't fully understand the mechanics of bonds, but if Young said it worked, it was good enough for me. However, we still had to get the money chairs to agree.

This was when I watched the sausage being made in the legislature. Negotiations for this matter came down to the last few hours on the last day of the legislative session. Usually that is a celebratory time, as the hard work has been done. Not for me and Young. While most of the other legislators were relaxing and partying, Young and I were sitting in the House Speaker's office, drinking with legislators to be polite, but waiting to be summoned by Senator Ige and Representative Luke to work out the final language on the bill to secure funding. We were waiting and waiting, and it was getting later and later. Finally, around 10 p.m., with a midnight deadline, Young and I were summoned to meet with Senator Ige.

Randall Nishimura, the bonding guru in the Department of the Attorney General, had coached me on the necessary wording that had to be in the bill to make it work. We had to explain to Senator Ige why his proposed wording was problematic but ours would work. Eventually we reached a compromise that worked, and the bill passed. I was grateful to chairs Ige and Luke for their cooperation and assistance. It had been a long evening, but we had closed the deal. As it turned out, the specific bond mechanism wording had to be redone the following year to take care of some technical legal issues, but the critical element of getting the legislature's commitment to funding the conservation easement had been achieved.

With the legislature's approval, we were able to fund and purchase a conservation easement on 665 acres of undeveloped land at Turtle Bay set aside for parks, trails and recreation, including the crown jewel, Kawela Bay. This included assistance from the City, the Trust for Public Land and the Nature Conservancy, who contributed additional funds to secure the $48.5 million deal. The governor held a press conference and signing ceremony at Kawela Bay. It was a lovely outing with the governor, the mayor, community groups, the Turtle Bay developer and TV cameras to show the public just what we had preserved. It was an important success for the Abercrombie administration to preserve this land for future generations. It was meaningful to me because I had gotten a chance to contribute and make a difference.

A Sticky Situation

Environmental problems come in many shapes and sizes—and globs. In September 2013, Matson Navigation Company, the largest shipping company bringing products to Hawai'i, spilled a massive amount of molasses in Honolulu Harbor—233,000 gallons, or 1,400 tons, enough to fill seven railroad tanker cars. Molasses is a thick, dark brown syrup obtained from raw sugar during the refining process. Matson stored the molasses in large tanks in the harbor area and loaded it onto ships through a network of pipes for transport to the mainland about once a week. This was a holdover from days of old, when sugarcane was the king of crops in Hawai'i. Matson knew about the leaking pipe but failed to repair it before it burst open in a fist-sized hole and discharged tons of molasses. Matson had experienced a similar molasses spill on Maui ten years before. But because molasses is not a regulated, hazardous substance, such as oil and gas, there was no regulatory framework for it.

The spill in the harbor was an environmental disaster. One might think that because it is a working harbor, there's nothing there—no marine life, no plant life. But in fact, Honolulu Harbor was home to numerous rare coral species and various fish and wildlife. All of that was wiped out by the molasses spill, turning the harbor area into a killing ground. The molasses did not disperse in the water like an oil spill. Instead, it settled to the bottom, sucking up all of the oxygen in the water, causing 26,000 fish and other marine species to die. Dead fish were floating to the surface for a couple of days. Divers reported that almost all sea life in the area died.

More importantly, the molasses coated many rare coral species that were growing in the harbor, killing them as well. Because corals provide homes to other fish and wildlife, they are critical habitat. Some of the corals can take hundreds of years to grow and were irreplaceable. Even before this spill, the coral reefs in Hawaiʻi were under threat from warming oceans and climate change. The spill made things worse.

It was ironic that this problem involved a spill of molasses, a by-product of sugar. Much of the development of Hawaiʻi is due to the rise of sugar in the 1800s. The growing climate of Hawaiʻi, the sunny temperate climate, abundance of rain and rich volcanic soils all combined to make Hawaiʻi a great place to grow sugar. Vast tracts of land were developed for sugarcane. They were made fertile through engineering creativity that constructed large irrigation ditches and flume systems that transported water from the wet windward sides to the vast open fields on the drier sides of the islands. Such engineering feats dramatically changed the landscape of Hawaiʻi.

We hired an environmental law firm to file suit against Matson. It was no small matter to sue Matson. Matson is a major Hawaiʻi company that provides a critical lifeline for food and goods needed by the community. Matson for many years has had the largest market share of shipping from the West Coast to Hawaiʻi and had generally been a good corporate citizen. But Matson had created the problem through negligence and needed to be held accountable.

In the last quarter of 2014, Matson wanted to settle the lawsuit. The uncertainty of the suit apparently had a negative effect on its stock price. Gov. Abercrombie told me that he had spoken to Matson, and he thought Matson would be willing to pay $10 million to settle the lawsuit. I checked with our environmental lawyers and experts.

The major damage to Hawai'i was the destruction of the corals. The fish and other wildlife would come back, but the corals took decades or centuries to grow and were already endangered. Coral reefs throughout the world have been under stress for decades due to global warming. A difference of a few degrees of extra heat in the oceans can mean the difference between life and death for coral reefs, as well as for the many species of fish and other wildlife that inhabit coral reefs. The lawyers and experts were clear that coral reefs are very difficult to regenerate, and thus it is quite expensive to try and regrow them. Their estimate was that the cost to replace the corals was $25 million or more, so that we should not settle for less.

But we were coming up to the end of Gov. Abercrombie's term and he wanted to settle the suit. The governor had been defeated in his reelection bid by Senator David Ige in the Democratic primary election in August 2014, so this was one of the last things that he could do. I regret it now, but I refused the governor. I had the statutory power to determine the settlement, and my lawyers and experts were telling me the claim was worth much more than Matson was willing to pay. I left office in December 2014 and left the resolution of the lawsuit to the next attorney general. In hindsight, I wish I had been more involved and actively tried to settle the case rather than leaving it to others.

Eight months later, in July 2015, my successor, Attorney General Doug Chin, announced a settlement of the lawsuit against Matson for a total of between $11.4 million and $15.4 million. This sounds like a better deal than the $10 million that Gov. Abercrombie had mentioned to me. However, the settlement actually only involved a payment of $5.9 million to the State, not $10 million. Matson was getting credit in the settlement for between $5.5 million and $9.5 million being spent by it to shut down all of their molasses facilities, tanks and pipes in Honolulu Harbor. But they had to do that anyway, and none of that money would go to the State.

Was this settlement better or worse than what Gov. Abercrombie had discussed with me? That's unclear and I'll never know. Matson may have intended the same thing in their conversation with Gov. Abercrombie. With more time and further investigation, our lawyers and experts may have revised their estimates upwards or downwards. Attorney General

Chin had the power and discretion to settle the suit as he saw fit and got a resolution that avoided years of litigation and uncertainty. I'm not going to second-guess him. Had I negotiated, I might have gotten a better or worse settlement. Those are what-ifs. My misgivings were simply that I had the chance to be in the room and make something happen, and I didn't.

Addressing issues relating to the preservation of the environment is critically important both for Hawaiʻi and for the world at large. The catastrophic effects of climate change and global warming are only beginning to be felt in large-scale ways, but such inexorable changes pose an existential threat to Hawaiʻi and its communities and underscore the interconnectedness of Hawaiʻi and the rest of the planet. Most importantly, the work was meaningful and purposeful because we were helping to preserve the land and the environment for future generations. It doesn't get better than that.

| 11 |

National Connections

The National Mortgage Crisis

Fear was in the air in 2008. The national mortgage crisis erupted then, and it and the ensuing Great Recession continued through the end of 2010, evaporating wealth and hitting the nation's communities with stunning force and speed. The financial world and the stock market as we knew it were crumbling and in free fall. People were losing their jobs, losing their homes. It was a brave new world and no one knew what was coming next, what to do or whom to trust.

In hindsight, of course, it was easy to see how the policies and politics of greed had led to a stunning debacle in banking and the spectacular burst of the housing bubble, causing ruin and despair for many. But at the time, few people realized that the nation's biggest banks and lending institutions had created a house of cards that would come tumbling down and bring everyone with it. The roots of the mortgage crisis are tangled indeed, but the main blame seems to lie with the combination of bad, even fraudulent, lending practices by bankers, and their ability to "securitize" mortgage loans to package and pass bad loans to others and avoid dealing with the problems they had created.

Home building has been a mainstay of the nation's economy for many years. What could be better than putting people in homes? For many years, the federal government has encouraged home construction and mortgage lending by banks to allow people to buy homes and build wealth. Long ago, banks would loan money to a homeowner and take a mortgage back on the home as security for payment of the loan. Over the years, a national system developed so that banks could sell those loans and mortgages to others, who then would take on the job and risk of collecting on specific loans and foreclosing on the mortgages if the loans were not paid. Securitization took that process one step further, bundling hundreds and thousands of mortgages together, using servicers to process the loans, and selling smaller pieces of the group of mortgages to others, spreading out the risk of collection. So far, so good.

But the bankers went off the deep end and laid the groundwork for the national mortgage crisis when they realized that securitization enabled them to substantially relax or ignore their loan requirements because they could pass the risk of nonpayment to a group of investors who were not even looking at the viability of the loans. The banks could get their money up front by creating the loans and mortgages and taking a fee, and then sell the loans and mortgages so that the risk of nonpayment became someone else's problem, not theirs.

The crisis arose when bankers started making riskier loans, to people and entities who would never be able to repay the loans, and then bundling and selling those crummy loans with good ones, so the risk of bad and fraudulent loans was hidden. There are legions of stories of loan officers who encouraged people to lie on their loan applications and claim income or money that they didn't have. Adjustable rate mortgages with large balloon payments that reset the loan terms to possibly unmanageable rates within a few years compounded the problems. All of this easy money fueled speculation and a rise in housing prices.

It was like the childhood card game where the queen of spades is passed around and around, and at the end of the game, whoever holds the queen of spades is the loser. When the housing bubble reached its peak, the banks holding the bad loans were stuck with them, the loans became due and people could not pay, the whole system came crashing down, assets and credit were frozen, jobs were lost, and the Great Recession was ushered in.

The National Association of Attorneys General (NAAG) was formed by state attorneys general in 1907 to discuss antitrust issues relating to Standard Oil Company. Over the years, NAAG has provided a platform for cooperation and concerted multistate action by state attorneys general.

In October 2010, a fifty-state Mortgage Foreclosure Multistate Group was formed and led by a committee of state attorneys general and banking regulators. The group investigated procedural defects involving foreclosures and the widespread process of lenders signing foreclosure documents without verifying their accuracy, a process known as "robo-signing," which called into question the validity of foreclosures and exposed the banks to substantial liability. The states allied with the federal government to bring the banks to account.

In 2012, the federal government and forty-nine state attorneys general, including Hawai'i's, reached a historic $25 billion agreement and consent judgment with the five largest mortgage servicers to address the foreclosure crisis and abuses. I was pleased to participate in this settlement and work with the other attorneys general to get this result. Hawai'i got over $71 million to be used for foreclosure relief, forgiveness and counseling for Hawai'i homeowners who were underwater on their mortgages. More importantly, the banks agreed to reform their mortgage servicing practices and adopt dozens of new common sense protections, such as requiring a single point of contact for borrowers and restricting "dual tracking" where lenders negotiated new payment plans while simultaneously pursuing foreclosures. These new procedures made the process much more consumer friendly and helped to reform the industry.

Sometimes the problems that confront our communities are larger than just one state or just one region. Sometimes those problems require concerted action from many like-minded people. Attorneys general have banded together to take on such problems for their states and the nation. Sometimes the action is litigation and lawsuits. Sometimes the action is regulation. Sometimes the action is merely the exchange of information and approaches. In the process of acting together, state attorneys general have created powerful networks capable of addressing national problems and creating national solutions.

Working with other attorneys general provided an opportunity to meet and interact with some tremendously capable and intelligent people on the national leadership and political stage, who have devoted themselves to making things better. Some were narrow, ideological politicians. But most were pragmatic problem solvers who were willing to work across partisan divides to forge solutions. This opportunity to work together with other state attorneys general as well as the federal government opened my eyes to the powers, prospects and possibilities that could be achieved through concerted, organized action.

NAAG and CWAG

NAAG is the largest of the attorney general organizations and includes the attorneys general of all fifty states, Washington, DC, and various territories such as Puerto Rico, Guam, American Samoa, the US Virgin Islands and the Northern Mariana Islands. Under NAAG's umbrella are conferences for the Eastern, Midwestern, Southern and Western regions. The Conference of Western Attorneys General (CWAG) is made up of the attorneys general from the "western" states, although CWAG has encouraged associate membership and attendance from all other states. A few years ago, CWAG formed a new group known as the Attorney General Alliance to serve as a larger national and international forum for bipartisan cooperation in the attorney general community.

The purpose of NAAG and the other conferences is to provide a forum for attorneys general to get together, exchange ideas and work collaboratively with one another. The meetings would raise cutting-edge issues and problems of mutual concern, such as antitrust matters, gambling, opioid addiction, sex trafficking, for-profit schools and payday lending. There would be presentations by experts in given areas, and opportunities for the attorneys general to ask questions and debate positions.

One of the interesting things about attending NAAG meetings was that everyone called the attorneys general by the title of "General." At my first meeting I was surprised to hear this. "Good morning, General." "How are you doing, General?" "How was your evening, General?" It was a strange introduction to the world of attorneys general. I thought I had stumbled into a meeting of the Joint Chiefs of Staff. The title struck me as odd because the phrase "attorney general" refers to an attorney who is a "general" attorney, meaning a generalist, not a specialist. The word "general" is an adjective, not a title. Instead of being attorneys specific, we are attorneys general. It would probably make a high school English teacher's head explode to hear an adjective being turned into a title and a noun, and attorneys general are not military officers in any sense of the word, but that's the reality of the situation when the rules of English are constantly being bent, modified and changed. Nonetheless, it's reportedly a practice that began a number of decades ago when Janet Reno was US attorney general, and the US Supreme Court justices would address her as "General." If it's good enough for the Supreme Court, it's good enough for me.

NAAG and CWAG are both bipartisan organizations that have tried to be even-handed in balancing Republican and Democratic sensibilities. In the hyper-partisan atmosphere of national politics today, that is a difficult task. There was also a Republican Attorneys General Association

(RAGA) and a Democratic Attorneys General Association (DAGA) that were clearly partisan organizations. However, my experience was that most of the attorneys general were interested in trying to work on common bipartisan solutions and focused on issues where partisan concerns were not as prominent.

NAAG and CWAG provided a tremendous opportunity for attorneys general like me, from small states such as Hawai‘i, to work with, break bread with and get to know other attorneys general in both political parties who were some of the up-and-coming leadership talent at the national level. The friendships that I made with my attorney general colleagues on both sides of the aisle were important to Hawai‘i, as I could quickly get critical information and cooperation by picking up a phone to call someone I knew and had a relationship with. For example, when Hawai‘i was facing an onslaught of video gambling machines being installed in strip malls, I got information from Ohio attorney general Mike DeWine about their efforts and techniques to combat this illegal enterprise. We also exchanged information with other states to identify and declare as illegal certain chemical formulations of synthetic marijuana products that were constantly being changed to skirt the laws.

NAAG has a number of committees that address national problems and concerns. When I became the chair of the NAAG Consumer Protection Committee, I was suddenly in demand for meetings, as various industries wanted to know if I was going to lead a charge against them. One memorable meeting I had was with an Indian tribe who wanted to become partners with a payday lender. Payday lenders provide small but quick loans to people who can't get normal credit or bank loans, charging them exorbitantly high interest rates, far higher than any credit card. Such rates can add up quickly, trapping the borrower into an endless cycle of paying off debt. Payday lenders are one of a range of institutions that are known as "poverty capital," that have evolved to profit from poor people. They argue that they are providing an essential service to people that banks won't service, and that their high interest rates merely reflect the increased risks of lending to customers with high default rates.

NAAG's Consumer Protection Committee and various attorneys general had investigated and taken action from time to time against payday lenders to limit interest rates that could be charged. While poor customers may need occasional cash as much as others, it has always seemed to me that they should not be penalized by egregiously high interest rates. My view was that payday lenders should be restricted to somewhat higher but still reasonable interest rates, so they did not get rich off the backs of the poor and people had a fighting chance to pay off their debt.

Some payday lenders had come up with a clever concept. Indian tribes are regarded as sovereign nations, with "sovereign immunity" from the laws of the states where they are located. A very clear example of this is gambling, where the federal courts have ruled that Indian casinos can operate on Indian land despite state prohibitions on gambling. Certain payday lenders wanted to "rent-a-tribe," i.e., partner with a tribe to run a payday lending operation that could claim they were outside the jurisdiction of state and federal law, thus making the tribe and the payday lender immune from regulation.

I met with the Indian tribe's representatives, along with the payday lender's representative and lobbyist. They wanted the Consumer Protection Committee and various attorneys general to look the other way if they operated in partnership with an Indian tribe. The tribe's representative pitched that such an operation would provide jobs and income for the tribe. Neither they nor the payday lender would answer my questions as to how much of the profits would be shared with the tribe, and whether the jobs and naming fee were merely nominal. I thought it was ironic that an Indian tribe, which probably had many poor members, was willing to join the poverty capital brigade and seek profit from the trials and tribulations of other poor people. My response was that although it appeared to be a clever concept, that wouldn't stop me or any other attorney general from prosecuting them if they broke state lending laws.

Attorneys general have engaged in concerted action at the national level for many years, bringing multistate investigations and lawsuits through NAAG to address various consumer protection issues, antitrust and unfair and deceptive advertising and commercial practices. Two notable lawsuits occurred when attorneys general sued Microsoft over monopolistic practices and separately brought suit against the four largest tobacco companies. The tobacco lawsuit led to a landmark settlement in 1998 with forty-six state attorneys general, providing for payments to the states of $206 billion over twenty-five years.

Many of the concerted activities by attorneys general seek to regulate or curtail bad behavior. I participated in one of the NAAG initiatives in this regard in 2013, when the NAAG Committee on Internet Privacy and Security sought to have Google make changes to its auto-complete programming. Google had an auto-complete feature that, as a person typed a Google query, would make suggestions to complete the query. The problem was that Google's auto-complete feature was at times making suggestions that were at times highly improper, leading users in directions that might be illegal. For example, innocent queries about drugs or driver's licenses might trigger an auto-complete suggestion for illegal drugs or fake driver's licenses. Queries about sex might trigger auto-complete suggestions for pornography, child pornography and highly suggestive and salacious entries.

Led by Mississippi attorney general Jim Hood, the Internet Committee sought meetings with Google representatives to request a solution. Google was very defensive and uncooperative until attorney general Hood threatened to issue Civil Investigative Demands (CIDs) and subpoenas of Google records. That got their attention, and Google representatives flew to meet with a group of attorneys general in Colorado. Unfortunately, Google's solution was not particularly satisfying, as Google claimed that the Communications Decency Act, a federal statute, shielded them from any liability or responsibility. Nonetheless, Google did agree to place substantially more people on a project to clean up and police the auto-complete function to eliminate inappropriate suggestions.

I also worked with other states and brought civil lawsuits in Hawai'i to address and punish bad behavior. In 2012, along with New Mexico and West Virginia, Hawai'i filed suit against seven major banks and credit card companies for "cramming" and "slamming"—unscrupulous, fraudulent practices against their own customers. These companies had run boiler room operations and offered "payment protection" plans that did very little for their customers, sometimes signing them up even when they refused, and failing to cancel even when the customers wanted out. The plans resulted in $15 to $30 monthly charges to millions of customers, who rarely noticed the charges, resulting in millions of dollars of profits. We settled the claims for substantial penalties to address the companies' bad behavior.

A newer development within the past couple of decades has been a rise in lawsuits brought by state attorneys general to challenge federal policies and actions in the political arena. Democratic attorneys general filed lawsuits against President George W. Bush to address various issues, including an attempt to force the Environmental Protection Agency

(EPA) to regulate greenhouse gases. When Barack Obama became president, Republican attorneys general filed numerous lawsuits for political purposes to stop or prevent various presidential initiatives regarding the Affordable Care Act, executive orders on immigration, EPA rules on carbon pollution, etc. The number of state attorney general lawsuits increased against President Obama.

Following the election of Donald Trump, Democratic attorneys general filed numerous lawsuits against new policies and actions put into place by President Trump. In 2018 in *Trump v. Hawaii*, my successor, Attorney General Douglas Chin, sued unsuccessfully to block President Trump's infamous Muslim travel ban. Other lawsuits by Democratic attorneys general have included challenges to the construction of President Trump's Mexican border wall, inaction by the EPA for violations of the Clean Water Act, changes in the policies of the Departments of Health and Human Services, and the Interior, over new rules and repeals of Obama era regulations, etc. Suits against the president by state attorneys general of the opposing political party have now become the new normal.

International Connections

Working with NAAG and CWAG also enabled me to make international connections with the attorneys general and top law enforcement officials of a few other nations. During my tenure, there were three countries—Israel, Taiwan and Turkey—that recognized that attorneys general of most states had decent prospects to become governors or US senators, and thus might be worth knowing. Israel and Taiwan had long-standing relationships with NAAG, inviting groups of attorneys general to visit their countries every couple of years and meet with leaders. Through the efforts of NAAG president Doug Gansler, Maryland's attorney general, Turkey also initiated such a relationship and hosted a few attorney general trips. CWAG has been the most active of the conferences, establishing a long-standing relationship with Mexico to help train Mexican prosecutors in trial techniques for drug trafficking cases, and recently developing similar relationships with some African nations.

I was privileged to visit Taiwan, Israel and Turkey on several attorney general trips. These were formal trips, almost government to government, involving a combination of tour activities and meetings with officials where we sipped tea and discussed world politics. In Taiwan, we met with President Ma Ying-jeou, various legislative leaders and prosecutors. In Israel, we met with former president Shimon Peres, a supreme court justice and other high government officials. In Turkey, we met with President Abdullah Gul and a supreme court justice, and we laid a wreath at the tomb of Kemal Ataturk, the founder of modern secular Turkey.

Since I am Chinese American, the Taiwanese government was quite happy to have me visit. I thought, perhaps naively, that the People's Republic of China might be similarly disposed and could be persuaded to host an attorney general trip to China. During my tenure, there had been a thawing in relationships and easing of military tensions between China and Taiwan, with more Cross-Strait (Taiwan Strait) relations and business, even though China has long claimed that Taiwan is part of China. I thought the timing might be auspicious. During the Asia-Pacific Economic Cooperation Economic Leaders' Meeting in Honolulu in 2011, I had made contacts with the Chinese Consul General based in Los Angeles. I followed up with letters and some meetings at the Chinese Consulate in Washington, DC, to suggest an attorney general tour to China. However, my efforts only resulted in a display of power politics by the Chinese government.

In 2012 and 2013, despite the thawing of diplomatic relations between China and Taiwan, China was starting to flex its soft power muscles to seriously try to isolate Taiwan in world politics. Using money and the promise of construction projects and contracts, China convinced approximately twenty nations in the world to renounce their diplomatic relationships with Taiwan, leaving Taiwan with few friends.

I learned about China's attempts to muscle Gov. Abercrombie in a similar manner. The Dalai Lama was invited to speak at the University of Hawai'i in April 2012. The Dalai Lama, an engaging, cheerful, cherubic Tibetan monk, is the spiritual and former political leader of Tibet, who was exiled in 1959 for leading an unsuccessful uprising against China. He is widely regarded as speaking with a voice of moral courage and certitude. Gov. Abercrombie knew the Dalai Lama from prior occasions and announced that they would meet. China, which occupies Tibet, has tried to control Tibet by installing its own version of the Dalai Lama. But China's attempts have been met with resistance and rejection by the Tibetan people. Because of the real Dalai Lama's profile and popularity, China has strongly objected to meetings by political leaders from other nations with the Dalai Lama, and unsuccessfully tried to discourage Gov. Abercrombie from his meeting.

Bruce Coppa, the governor's chief of staff, told me that in an effort to discourage the meeting, China had suddenly and unexpectedly scheduled a meeting around the same time between Gov. Abercrombie and a high-level Chinese official who was ranked number five in the Central Politburo of the Chinese Communist Party. China communicated that this person was on his way back to China from Peru, planned to stop in Honolulu, and wanted to meet with Gov. Abercrombie, coincidentally just before the Dalai Lama's appearance. A week or so before the meeting, a Chinese representative came to see the governor and demanded loudly that the governor not meet with the Dalai Lama. The governor tried to explain that in Hawaiʻi, with the spirit of aloha, all visitors are welcome, and since he personally knew the Dalai Lama, it was only polite to meet with him. The Chinese representative angrily rejected this reasoning and continued to demand that the governor cancel the meeting. The governor refused. When the high-ranking Chinese official showed up in Honolulu, he canceled his visit with the governor at the last minute, saying he was suddenly "ill."

Although I was aware of this background, I was still naively optimistic that the Chinese government might want to start a relationship with attorneys general and NAAG. I enlisted the help of retired rear admiral James McPherson, who was then the executive director of NAAG, and was subsequently appointed as the United States Under Secretary of the Army during President Trump's term of office. McPherson told me he met with a Chinese consulate official, who said China would be happy to "discuss" hosting an attorney general trip, but if and only if NAAG first severed all relations with Taiwan. Amazing. China thought that NAAG would be willing to cut off Taiwan just for the pleasure of "talking" to China about a trip. Soft power? Sometimes people and nations act in sophisticated and subtle ways. At other times they are just as clumsy as junior high school kids trying to bully one another. This was one of those times. I was disappointed but not surprised.

My experience with NAAG, CWAG and the other national attorneys general and public officials was an unexpected but illuminating window on the national political scene, national issues of concern to many states and an opportunity to interact with some of the up-and-coming leaders in our country. I met many outstanding people on both sides of the political aisle who will have a voice and make decisions to guide the future of the nation. While there were sharp ideological and political differences among my colleagues, I was pleasantly surprised to find many attorneys general who were willing to put aside partisan differences to work collaboratively to get things done. NAAG also provided an opportunity to engage with international leaders and observe both subtle and not so subtle handling of international affairs. I hope it is not naive, but these experiences made me optimistic that we can overcome the current climate of divisiveness and work together to find solutions to the problems we face. We deserve no less. ❦

| 12 |

Fun Stuff

Government really is serious business, but being attorney general was not always grim and humorless. There were many wonderful, fun and serendipitous experiences, with lots of laughs, delight and joy. The following are a few of those moments.

Cloak and Dagger

Politics is a game played with very few rules. But it is deadly serious because there is so much power, responsibility, policy and money at stake. This is true at the state level and even truer at the national level. Politicians and other participants sometimes feel free to make up their own rules and facts to try to build themselves up and drag their opponents down. While it would be nice if politicians were ethical and always told the truth, the fact is that for some people, the truth and facts are nothing more than suggested guidelines that they feel free to ignore.

In 2011, President Barack Obama was facing an election in 2012 that was by no means assured. He was under constant attack from Republicans, and many of the attacks were not principled, reasoned policy debates. Instead they were crazy, racist, thinly veiled dog-whistle coded falsehoods from right-wing nut jobs, who claimed that President Obama was born in Kenya, that he was not an American citizen and that, therefore, he could not properly serve as president. President Obama had in fact been born in Honolulu, Hawai'i, where he grew up. Sadly, that fact mattered little in the political narrative, and one of the principal proponents of these despicable lies was Donald J. Trump, who rode those and other falsehoods to become president of the United States in 2016.

In 2011, Trump and others kept repeating their racist trope and demanded that President Obama produce his birth certificate. The State of Hawai'i had already released a statement that President Obama had been born in Hawai'i and had a birth certificate, but that had not quelled the furor of the far right. Birth certificates are personal, private records, so the State could not release the birth certificate itself but continued to affirm that it existed. Moreover, birth certificates from 1961, when President Obama was born, were kept by the Department of Health (DOH) in large bound handwritten volumes, which were held under lock and key and not easily accessed. The original birth certificates of that era were not electronic and were not loose papers. I had not even seen the original volume, although others in my office had.

You might think that the truth would be sufficient to shut down this trope. You would be wrong. The repeated vehemence of the lie continued to fuel the far-right conspiracy theorists and opportunistic politicians like Trump. President Obama's team decided to release a copy of the real birth certificate. I got a call from a lawyer from Perkins Coie, a law firm that was President Obama's personal counsel. She said this was very hush-hush, but that she wanted to fly out to Hawai'i and pick up a copy of President Obama's birth certificate, so it could be released to the media.

We made arrangements to copy the birth certificate. Because these records were in the basement of the DOH, Jill Nagamine, one of the deputy attorneys general, went to verify the bound volume and the copy, to make sure it was accurate. The lawyer flew to Hawai'i, and I met her at the Prince Hotel. I handed her the copies of President Obama's birth certificate. It felt very cloak and dagger.

As I was handing her the documents, I noticed that there were some very faint numbers marked on the copy of the birth certificate, for which I had no explanation. This was somewhat disconcerting, because I felt that if we had any unexplained matters, they could become fodder for the right-wing nut jobs. What did these numbers mean? Would someone claim they were code for "Born in Kenya?" I immediately called to find out the explanation, in case this question was raised by the media. It turned out that these were simply computer codes that had been used to transfer the information from the old birth certificates to the DOH computer system, not a sinister secret code.

A couple of days later, President Obama's team announced that his birth certificate was being posted on his website. Of course, the right-wing nut jobs discounted these as forgeries and continued to spew their nonsense. It should have laid the whole controversy to rest, but it did not.

Instead, the flat-out lies and the overt racism against President Obama continued to persist throughout the 2012 election campaign, fueled by people such as Trump. Liars are rarely bothered by the truth. Fortunately for the country, President Obama was reelected in 2012 and served another four years.

Governator for a Day

In Hawai'i, the attorney general is second in line to take over the helm of government if something happens or the governor leaves the state. The lieutenant governor is first in line, and often serves as acting governor when official or other duties require the governor to be out of state. When both the governor and the lieutenant governor leave the state, the attorney general becomes the acting governor, with full plenipotentiary powers. At least in theory. Of course, if the attorney general started issuing decrees and making drastic changes, as soon as the governor or lieutenant governor returned, those powers would evaporate and any pronouncements, pardons or decrees would be subject to instant reversal. Since the State acts through many persons, if the attorney general started taking unusual actions that others thought seemed off, it's highly likely that people would pay him or her no mind, and then call the governor to set things right.

The opportunity to sit in the governor's chair and take over as the head of state was more ceremonial than real. But it is not nothing, and it's certainly possible to make some things happen. My predecessor, Mark Bennett, who is now a United States Ninth Circuit Court of Appeals judge, took the opportunity to issue an official proclamation declaring a certain day as "New York Yankees Day" in Hawai'i in honor of his favorite baseball team. I'm not sure how the New York Mets or Boston Red Sox fans in Hawai'i took this, if they even knew about it. I imagine that Bennett had cleared this action in advance with then-governor Linda Lingle, but it's certainly possible that he simply seized the opportunity and acted decisively.

I was the acting governor of Hawai'i three times. It was great, but it sounds a lot more important than it was.

The first time I became acting governor was in my first year on the job. The governor's office called me on a Thursday or Friday informing me that both the governor and lieutenant governor would have overlapping travel out of state, so that I would be the guy in charge for about ten or twelve hours on a Saturday. That's when I first learned that I was second in line. Of course, that got me thinking: What did I really get to do as acting governor?

In Hawai'i, both the governor and the lieutenant governor have security details—big, burly, capable guys who have arms as big as my legs and can handle many different situations. They both get driven around in big black Chevy Suburban SUVs, as befits their status. As attorney general, I did not have such a security detail or transportation perks, although some other state attorneys general do. The first two questions I asked were, "Do I get a security detail? And will they drive me around in a black SUV?" I figured I could ride around, see how it felt to be an important guy and visit some of my friends to duly impress them with my newly elevated status. No such luck. The governor's office said, "No way. No security detail. No black SUV. Just go home and pray that nothing happens. If something does happen, we'll call you."

That Saturday, while I was acting governor, nothing changed. I certainly didn't feel any different and didn't do anything out of the ordinary. No one called for my gubernatorial advice or pronouncements. I just spent that Saturday at home, and Johanna, my wife, told me to take out the gubernatorial trash—which I did, since I appreciate the power of authority and direction.

The second time I became acting governor was about six months later. I again got a call that both the governor and the lieutenant governor would be traveling, so that I was the guy. Again it was on a Thursday or Friday that I got the call, and again I was to be the number one official in the state of Hawai'i over the weekend. Once again, I asked my two key questions. "Do I get a security detail? And can they drive me around in a black Suburban?" Once again, the governor's office gave me the same refrain. "No way. No security detail. No black SUV. Just go home and pray that nothing happens." So once again I went home. This time I took out the gubernatorial trash without Johanna having to ask me. Sometimes I can be independent and decisive.

The third time I became acting governor I had been in office for a couple of years. This time I got the call early in the week and was told I'd be the acting governor on that Friday. I decided to do things a little differently. Since I knew the answers already, I didn't need to ask whether I'd get a security detail or a black SUV. Instead I was left to my own devices. I didn't have a favorite baseball team or a burning desire to make a proclamation, so I decided to throw a party. Independent and decisive? Perhaps. Using the full plenipotentiary powers of the government?

Hardly. But if I was going to serve as the acting governor, I figured we should at least try and mark the occasion with a little fun.

My secretary, Ann Nishihira, found an online copy of an old Arnold Schwarzenegger film poster for *The Terminator*, and we Photoshopped my face in and changed the title to "The Governator" for the party invitations. I made commemorative party favor cards. On one side was a copy of a Monopoly "Get Out of Jail Free" card, and on the backside I signed them as The Governator, making the cards effective only during the day, which would have expired at the time of the party. I invited a bunch of my friends, my staff, deputy attorneys general, the governor's chief of staff, some members of the cabinet and other attorneys to celebrate with me. After I had worked a full day as acting governor, we took over a section of a bar in Restaurant Row and had a grand time, as befits the office. I passed out my "Get Out of Jail Free" cards as an "official" party favor. My son, Ryan, and his friends donned black T-shirts and black jeans, put in earpieces and served as my security detail, so I could check off that box. Still no black SUV. Some things are just not meant to be.

That Friday was the last time I served as acting governor. I like to think that it was simply a coincidence that for the remainder of my term the governor and the lieutenant governor did not happen to travel outside Hawaiʻi at the same time. Or perhaps the governor's office heard about my Governator party, became concerned about what might happen if I took the reins a fourth time, and managed their travel schedules to avoid such a possibility. Unlikely. But not impossible.

The Wonder Blunder

One of the great things about being attorney general is that sometimes you get to meet and talk to some very famous and interesting people. I have been privileged to meet and exchange ideas with US senators and congresspersons, US Supreme Court justices and even international political leaders. But by far, my all-time greatest day for meeting famous people was a day in February 2013 when I met Stevland Morris, known to the world as Stevie Wonder.

The day started out with a bang. I was in Washington, DC, for the annual winter meeting of the National Association of Attorneys General. That morning, Vice President Joseph Biden met with us for a half hour, giving an impassioned speech about the need for more and better gun control. He then worked the room to meet and chat with each of us individually. After lunch, a smaller group of attorneys general who were part of the Conference of Western Attorneys General (CWAG) went to meet with the ambassador to the United States from Mexico. He was the former attorney general of Mexico and had worked with CWAG for a number of years on a joint project training Mexican prosecutors to prosecute drug traffickers. Our group of CWAG attorneys general then went to meet with Ken Salazar, the United States Secretary of the Interior. Secretary Salazar had previously served as the attorney general of Colorado and had been a member of CWAG.

That evening, I dined with Brian Schatz, one of Hawai'i's new US senators. I had worked closely with Senator Schatz over the past two years, when he was the lieutenant governor of Hawai'i before being appointed by Gov. Neil Abercrombie to fill the vacant Senate seat left open by the recent death of Senator Daniel Inouye. Joining us for dinner were Andy Winer, Senator Schatz's chief of staff, and Margery Bronster, a former Hawai'i attorney general.

After dinner, Bronster and I took a cab back to the hotel and decided to have a drink in the bar. After a few minutes, Dustin McDaniel, the attorney general of Arkansas, and his wife, Bobbi, came into the bar and joined us. A couple of glasses of wine later, suddenly Bobbi said, "Hey, Stevie Wonder just walked into the bar!" We tried not to be too obvious as we craned our heads around to see that Stevie (although it may seem overly familiar to refer to Stevie as Stevie, that has not stopped me) had indeed come in and was sitting at a table in a corner, along with a number of people in his entourage. The light over his table had been turned off by the bar, perhaps to provide him with more privacy. McDaniel said he knew and had met Stevie, and after a few minutes he got up and walked over to Stevie's table to say hello. McDaniel is a really friendly and gregarious guy, and he spent several minutes talking to Stevie before retiring for the night. I then got up and went to the restroom outside of the bar, which necessitated walking past Stevie's table.

Now for a little (actually, more than a little) backstory. About six months earlier, Stevie Wonder's name had been associated with a scandal at the University of Hawai'i, although Stevie was blameless. A couple of scam artists had convinced some lower level officials at UH that they represented Stevie and could deliver him to do a UH benefit concert on campus. Of course, Stevie Wonder is a true megastar, and the idea that he would come to UH had everyone giddy with anticipation. The lower level officials pushed the idea up the chain to successively higher officials, all the way up to the director of athletics and the Office of General Counsel, who both approved the concept and arrangements.

Somehow no one at UH thought to check out the bona fides of the scam artists, whether they really did represent Stevie or if they could do what they said, before charging ahead at full speed. UH wired $200,000 to the scam artists' bank account in Florida and announced in the media that there would be a Stevie Wonder concert within a couple of weeks to benefit UH Athletics.

This announcement set off an absolute frenzy in Hawai'i. Everybody and his mother wanted a ticket to the hottest concert event to come along in quite a while. Since it would benefit UH Athletics, which was in the red, it would be a win-win situation! Unfortunately, the frenzy did not pass me by. I arranged to buy fourteen floor tickets for myself and a group of friends.

The bubble of my happiness and that of the Hawai'i community lasted about one day before it burst and disintegrated into finger pointing and recriminations. It turned out that Stevie's actual agent, Creative Artists Agency (CAA), based in Los Angeles, heard about the concert and called UH to inform them that CAA was Stevie's real agent, and that neither they nor Stevie had heard of or approved of this concert, and that there was no way it was going to happen. Thud! The bubble of happiness became a lead balloon that hit the floor and burst apart, creating collateral damage everywhere.

UH immediately issued a retraction and mea culpa, promising to refund all the monies that had been taken in. The papers started calling it "the Wonder Blunder." The $200,000 wire transfer had vanished into the wind, and after a few lame attempts to reassure the public that they really did represent Stevie, so did the scam artists, although they were eventually caught and prosecuted.

M. R. C. Greenwood, the university's president, promptly suspended her athletic director and placed him on paid leave pending an investigation. Although the investigation immediately cleared the AD, since he had been out of town when the final paperwork was signed and the $200,000 was sent, Greenwood never reinstated him. This incensed many legislative leaders, who liked him and called for accountability. The athletic director threatened a lawsuit for damage to his reputation and eventually reached a settlement with UH for a newly created three-year job with unclear duties paying substantially more money. The AD accepted the new position, but then soon departed for a job at another school.

The State Senate convened an investigative hearing about the mishandling of both the Stevie Wonder concert and the personnel snafu with the athletic director, grilling the school's president for a couple of days. She revealed that UH had spent more than $1 million in attorney's fees to investigate the matter. She was grumpy and defensive and six months later resigned for "personal" reasons.

All of this background was firmly in my mind (more or less) as I walked back to my table in the DC restaurant. As I walked by Stevie's table, I was feeling somewhat emboldened, perhaps due to the glasses of wine I had consumed, and I thought, as I have occasionally done, *What the heck, what could possibly go wrong?* I promptly made a left turn to take me directly to Stevie's table. As I approached and almost reached the table, I could see that Stevie had headphones on and was talking into a small microphone for his cellphone. One of his entourage stood up and raised both hands to me and said, "Look, this is a private party and we would prefer if you don't disturb us." Not unexpected. So I opened my hands, palms up, in a hopefully sincere gesture and went into a hastily improvised speech.

"Sure," I said, "I don't want to bother you, but I was just sitting with my friend Dustin McDaniel, the attorney general of Arkansas, who chatted with you a few minutes ago. I'm David Louie, the attorney general of the state of Hawai'i, and I just wanted to apologize to Mr. Wonder on behalf of the people and the state of Hawai'i for the problems that we had in Hawai'i a few months ago and the fact that Mr. Wonder's name was dragged through the mud through no fault of his own, but simply because we had some scam artists who took the University of Hawai'i for a couple of hundred thousand. I just wanted to take the opportunity to say that we in Hawai'i are very, very sorry, and I won't bother you further."

I stopped speaking and was about to go back to my table when I heard Stevie say into his microphone, "I'll talk to you later," and then he took off his headphones and he reached his right hand across the table toward me. Wonder of wonders! (In so many ways!) I reached out and shook his hand. And then he said, "You know, I heard about that thing, and I was thinking that maybe there might be something that we could do to make it right."

This simple statement started me off on a chain of events and interactions that were simply serendipitous. At the time, I took it as an opening to immediately suggest that if Mr. Wonder (I did not want to press my luck by presuming to address him by the familiar "Stevie") would be willing to consider it, I would do all I could in my power as attorney general to make arrangements for an actual Stevie Wonder concert in Honolulu put on by a real concert promoter in Hawai'i, Tom Moffatt, who had produced shows in Hawai'i for Stevie, Elvis and Michael Jackson, among many others, and was the real deal, and someone I had worked with before. I told him that I would enlist the aid of Gov. Abercrombie. I did probably go over the line of plausibility and suggest that I thought I might even try to arrange a cameo appearance for Mr. Wonder on the hit television show *Hawaii Five-0*, since I had recently met the executive producer of the show.

I was willing at that point to promise my mother or my firstborn if I could somehow seal the deal. In any event, I tap danced for all I was worth for a few minutes, talking about how this would be a tremendously redemptive event for the people and state of Hawai'i, since the scam had made UH and the people of the Islands look like fools. Eventually I ran out of things to say. Stevie said that he would be interested in hearing more, so I exchanged business cards with two of the guys at the table, gave Stevie a Hawai'i attorney general challenge coin with the state seal on it, which I happened to be carrying, and went back to my table to tell Bronster what had just happened.

After a short while I went back to my hotel room, where I proceeded to call first my wife, and then the governor, to tell them of my serendipitous day and how this chance meeting might be the start of a beautiful friendship. Both expressed the thought that if I were able to make a Stevie Wonder concert happen, it would be a really cool thing. The governor pledged his support to this effort.

Over the ensuing months I reached out and got to know Matt Ater, one of Stevie's friends who was with him that night, who had given me his business card. Ater, a partially sighted technology whiz who lives in the Washington, DC, area, had helped out Stevie with assistive technology, became friends with him and had been simply getting together with Stevie when I met them.

I talked to Ater about the whole Wonder Blunder and ensuing mess that had occurred in Hawai'i, how bad UH had looked, and how there were many people here who would love to attend a Stevie Wonder concert. I arranged for Gov. Abercrombie to talk to Ater to express his personal interest in having Stevie consider doing a concert in Hawai'i. I offered to fly up to Los Angeles to meet with Stevie to further discuss the matter, and we were trying to coordinate some times and dates. I also contacted Tom Moffatt, who was extremely interested in promoting a concert and contacted Stevie's agent about adding Honolulu to a possible world tour for Stevie. I stayed in touch with Ater, who told me that Stevie had continued to express interest in the idea of a concert. However, I was not able to make any concrete arrangements.

Then serendipity came again. Johanna and I were on Maui in October 2013, helping to host a CWAG conference on digital privacy. Marty Jackley, the attorney general of South Dakota and the then-chair of CWAG, had wisely chosen to have the event in Maui rather than in Sioux Falls, South Dakota. About fifteen attorneys general and some 100 people were at the conference. CWAG had arranged for me to host a deep-sea fishing charter for Saturday, the day after the conference ended, to try and land a large marlin, at the personal request of Jackley and Wayne Stenehjem, the attorney general of North Dakota. Stenehjem's stated goal was to catch a fish one inch longer than Jackley's. We had a couple of boats all ready to go out on Saturday morning.

On Thursday evening, Johanna and I had dinner with Dustin McDaniel and his wife Bobbi, along with Catherine Cortez-Masto, the attorney general of Nevada, who is now one of Nevada's US senators, and her husband, Paul Masto. We were swapping stories and exchanging laughs when McDaniel brought up my encounter with Stevie Wonder. Of course, I recounted the whole story and McDaniel's prominent role, and we all had a good laugh.

The next morning, while I was sitting next to McDaniel in a CWAG panel presentation being led by Cortez-Masto about digital and Internet privacy, I got a text message from Ater. "Stevie is doing a private concert in Hawai'i on Saturday and would like you to come." I thought this would be a great opportunity to connect with Stevie and try and cement plans for a public concert, as we had discussed. I immediately showed the text to McDaniel, who texted Cortez-Masto in the middle of her presentation. We all tried to keep from laughing.

I immediately told Ater, "Yes! Also, can I bring Johanna?" I am slow but not totally clueless. Ater was pretty sure Johanna could come but did not have any further details on the concert. Where in Hawai'i? What island? What time? I called Johanna, and she set to Internet sleuthing, shortly coming up with some of the answers. Only hours before, a media story had broken that Larry Ellison, Internet billionaire and owner of Oracle and the island of Lāna'i, was putting on a private Stevie Wonder concert in Waikīkī for Oracle's top sales producers.

We now had to make changes in our plans. There was no time to go deep-sea fishing and fly back to Honolulu from Maui in time for the concert. I told Jackley and the others that an opportunity had come along that I could not pass up, and they were on their own. McDaniel told me he had been "better dealed" by more prominent people than me but acknowledged that he would have thrown me under the bus if our positions were reversed.

On Saturday morning I woke up at dawn to see the attorneys general off on their deep-sea fishing trip and wish them luck in landing a record-setting marlin. Unfortunately, they did not see a single fish on the whole trip, but I did not learn that until later. Johanna and I then flew back to O'ahu and went to the concert. Shameless groupies!

The concert that night was fabulous! We obtained backstage passes and got to hang with the band members and Stevie's staff while waiting for the concert to begin. We were privileged to participate in a prayer circle with Stevie and the band just before the concert began. What a great moment! We then followed Stevie and the band to the back of the stage and had seats on the side. Johanna gave Stevie a fragrant *pīkake* lei that he initially wore, then decided to hang on the center microphone stand because it was interfering with his microphone pickup. Stevie played for an hour and a half straight, and he and the band were great!

Afterwards, Johanna and I met with Stevie and his new wife and baby in his trailer for a half hour. I gave him a wooden bowl I had made from koa wood. We thanked him for including us in this truly special occasion. At one point the saxophone player came into the trailer and began scat singing with Stevie for a few minutes. I then pitched Stevie in earnest about how the governor and I wanted to facilitate a public UH benefit concert for him in Honolulu as a redemptive moment to make up for the prior blunders of the UH. Stevie told me he was willing to do such a concert and would be happy to help. What a night!

Unfortunately, try as I might, I was unable to make a Stevie Wonder concert happen in Hawai'i. A few months later I spoke with Stevie's CAA agent, a high-powered Hollywood type who let me know that despite the Ellison concert, it was too expensive and time consuming for Stevie to put on a concert in Hawai'i unless it was part of an international concert tour and Hawai'i was added as a stop. Sadly, this never materialized. But it was not for lack of trying.

My encounters with Stevie Wonder were the highlight of the fun things I got to do as attorney general. There were many serious moments, and many lighthearted and serendipitous moments. It was a privilege to participate in all of them. ❦

| 13 |

The Beginning of the End

The mood was somber and resigned in the Abercrombie for Governor headquarters on August 9, 2014, the night of the Democratic primary election. Despite a gigantic war chest advantage, the support of many major unions, the endorsements of politicians and the efforts of countless volunteers, the polling had been ominously bad for weeks, even months. Faithful cabinet officials, government employees, staffers and volunteers had gathered at headquarters over familiar pizza, chili, and stew and rice meals to watch the primary election returns, and no one was joyous or celebrating. As the initial election returns reported on TV showed a large and substantial lead for the challenger, the state senator David Ige, a hollow feeling descended on the room. I had that same feeling, as we all took the loss personally.

It was a sad moment, and not just because people would have to look for new jobs and change their lives. It was sad because although much had been accomplished, the work was still unfinished; the comprehensive New Day vision that Gov. Abercrombie and his team had ushered in had only just begun and certainly was not completed. The opportunity for this team to effect change for the better in state government was slipping away and would soon be gone.

The campaign had tried, had worked mightily to give Gov. Abercrombie a second four-year term, but had come up short. There was tremendous talent on the governor's reelection campaign staff, led by experienced hands like Harry Mattson and Bill Kaneko. Gov. Abercrombie had successfully won many political races in Hawai'i over forty years and had an incredible network of supporters and helpers. Mattson and the team had deployed a well-organized effort to communicate the governor's message and get out the vote.

The campaign had garnered substantial donations from the usual sources, building a war chest of over $4 million, ten times that of the challenger, which was deployed through nicely scripted TV commercials and other media outlets. Giant tent campaign rallies had been held with musicians, politicians and stew and rice, although to smaller crowds than had come out in 2010, when the governor first was elected. Phone banks of volunteers had worked long hours to call Democratic voters to support the governor.

Even I, who generally hated political campaigning, had gone out on a few weekends with teams to conduct neighborhood canvassing, hanging flyers on door knockers of targeted Democratic voters based on computer printouts of voting data. I did so because I thought Gov. Abercrombie and his team had done a great job. Besides, I liked being attorney general and wanted to continue, if that was in the cards.

Gov. Abercrombie and the campaign team ran a good, strong, principled campaign, one that emphasized his achievements, his New Day Vision, the improvements that had been made, the initiatives he had championed. The Abercrombie campaign did not go negative in any way, shape or form. Although other political campaigns in Hawaiʻi have gone negative, sometimes simply fabricating rumors to smear the other side, and some consultants have suggested that going negative might have won the campaign, Gov. Abercrombie was not that kind of politician. He had a strong record of exemplary public service and proven leadership and ran on that basis.

I helped to prepare Gov. Abercrombie for his TV debates with Senator Ige. We held a number of sessions where we cross-examined the governor, pounced on his answers and got him ready for those encounters. We reviewed long reports of opposition research on both Gov. Abercrombie and Senator Ige, looking for vulnerabilities, inconsistencies, foibles and the thousand and one little details that can get brought up in a political campaign. There were not many gotcha tidbits in those reports, as both men were pretty squeaky clean as politicians. Gov. Abercrombie was on his game and prepared in those debates. He more than held his own, but it was not enough.

A few days before the primary election, Hurricane Iselle, which reached Category 4 hurricane status before dropping down to a moderate tropical storm, made landfall on the Big Island. It downed hundreds of trees, blocking roads and toppling power lines, and caused millions of dollars of damage. The governor issued an emergency proclamation, and special voting arrangements had to be made in certain precincts because of limited road access and an inability to open certain polling places. The governor had me, rather than himself, as the public face on TV to explain these governmental efforts, to avoid any criticism that he was trying to politically profit from the crisis. Other politicians have seen their popularity increase in times of crisis and emergencies, but that did not happen here.

So why did the governor lose? Why was Neil Abercrombie the first incumbent governor in Hawaiʻi to lose a primary race since 1962?

One of my friends, former Oklahoma attorney general Mike Turpen (campaign slogan—"It's Turpen Time"), who ran numerous political campaigns, used to tell me, "The candidate whose personal qualities and attributes best meet up with the wants and needs of the electorate on the day of the election is the one who wins." While Gov. Abercrombie's personal qualities and attributes were winners in 2010, they were not in 2014.

From my perspective, although I'm far from a seasoned political pro, there were several reasons why this occurred. To me, the biggest factor in sowing the seeds of destruction was the fiscal dilemma Gov. Abercrombie walked into when he took office, combined with his early efforts to raise money to comply with the constitutional mandate of having a balanced state budget, which angered many constituents who were not willing to forgive him. Although Gov. Abercrombie liked to say that the first year was only the first quarter of the game with three more quarters to go, his solid accomplishments for the State later in his term were just not sufficient to overcome the personal antipathy that arose among teachers and others who felt financially threatened by the governor's early initiatives. Another factor was that Gov. Abercrombie, although a charming man on many occasions, did not always come off as warm, fuzzy and likeable. Instead, sometimes he came off as one of the smartest guys in the room, and one who did not suffer fools gladly. As we all know from junior high school, being the smartest guy in the room does not guarantee a win in popularity contests.

Finally, another factor was Hawaiʻi's racial composition with a large Japanese American component, and the fact that Senator Ige is Japanese American. I don't believe this was an overriding factor here, as Gov. Abercrombie had gotten substantial support from Japanese Americans in the past, and many white politicians in Hawaiʻi have been elected over other Japanese American candidates. But that aspect of the electorate cannot be dismissed. Others have written that a key factor was

Gov. Abercrombie's refusal of the deathbed request by the late US senator Daniel K. Inouye to appoint Representative Colleen Hanabusa as his successor. In my view, that event was not the key factor, as Senator Schatz beat Representative Hanabusa in a close head-to-head special election for the Senate seat at the same time as the primary.

The Fiscal Dilemma

There is never enough money to do everything you want to do. Never. When I first joined Gov. Abercrombie's administration in 2011, I began reading the commentaries of political pundits and analysts, who wrote about the dilemma confronting progressive governors in this era. In 2011, we were still in the throes of the Great Recession, which had begun in 2008. The commentators uniformly said that progressive governors—and Neil Abercrombie was certainly progressive—were confronted with a stark choice. They could "feed the beast," meaning satisfy the salary and benefit demands of public unions, or they could implement new progressive programs or initiatives to address pressing problems in the community, but they could not do both. There was simply not enough money.

Gov. Abercrombie was immediately confronted with this dilemma. The legislative session for 2011 began in mid-January, only a month after Gov. Abercrombie was sworn in. This first legislative session was all about trying to achieve fiscal responsibility. Gov. Abercrombie had inherited a government that was fiscally underwater and in the red by $400 million, or about 4% of the annual state budget.

Gov. Linda Lingle, Gov. Abercrombie's predecessor, had had a very difficult time because there was not enough money from tax collections to finance government services, let alone finance government programs. In June 2009, Lingle announced that all state workers would take three furlough days a month for the next two years—a 13.8% pay cut—to reduce a projected budget deficit of $2 billion over two years. Three government unions filed a lawsuit to block the plan. After negotiations, the "Furlough Fridays" were reduced to two days a month. Without state workers on the job, schools, agencies and state offices were closed, meaning that the state services people had come to rely on were not available. This was an unmitigated and very unpopular economic disaster. People who depended on government programs and services suddenly had to fend for themselves to determine what to do. Parents had to figure out how to take care of their kids who were suddenly no longer in school on certain Fridays.

Gov. Abercrombie did not want to repeat the mistakes of the Lingle administration. But because the State was still fiscally underwater by hundreds of millions of dollars, something had to be done. Gov. Abercrombie decided to impose a 5% pay cut rather than furloughs or cutting back of labor hours. All government officials and employees, including himself, all cabinet officers and staffers, were subject to the 5% pay cut.

Gov. Abercrombie had negotiated this pay cut with two of the three major government unions before making the announcement—the Hawaii Government Employees Association (HGEA) and the United Public Workers (UPW). The HGEA was the largest government employees' union, and they agreed first, but the price of getting such an agreement was that they got a "most favored nations" clause. In labor negotiation terms, a most favored nations clause meant that if the government later agreed to better or more favorable terms with another union, then the HGEA members would also get the benefit of such terms. If the State did not get agreement or impose the 5% pay cut on everyone else, it would have to give back the 5% to the HGEA members. This gave the HGEA comfort that they would not look foolish for having agreed to something that other unions did not accept. But it also tied the hands of the government negotiators in dealing with the other unions, because it meant that the administration would have no room to move if the other unions held out for more. That is exactly what happened.

The Hawaii State Teachers Association (HSTA) would not agree to the 5% pay cut. Hawai'i's government is a little unusual in the US in that it administers the public educational system and schools in Hawai'i. While many other states have schools that are administered at the county level, all public schools in Hawai'i are administered by the State. All teachers in Hawai'i were thus state employees and part of the HSTA. The teachers decided that they were not going to take a 5% pay cut. As was stated by one of them to the news media, they were better and more important than the "cone droppers," the state construction workers who helped to drop cones to mark contraflow lanes for traffic control in the mornings.

Gov. Abercrombie then had no choice but to impose the 5% pay cut on the teachers. This made them angry and contentious, and it alienated a large number of potential voters. A lawsuit was brought unsuccessfully by the HSTA to prevent the 5% pay cut from being imposed. Contentious and bitter labor negotiations and litigation with the HSTA over a new collective bargaining agreement began and dragged on for years.

Because the HSTA would not agree to the pay cut, and because the State was still underwater and in the red, Gov. Abercrombie had to go to the legislature with a number of initiatives to try to shore up the State's finances. Gov. Abercrombie introduced a bill to tax pensions. Although pensions are taxed in a number of other states, they had not previously been taxed in Hawai'i. This measure proved highly unpopular with senior citizens and the powerful American Association of Retired Persons (AARP). The governor also had to hold the line on the budgets for grants-in-aid and program disbursements for needy, vulnerable and poor people. This did not make him popular with those who depended on government funds.

Gov. Abercrombie tried to appeal to the sound fiscal sense of the electorate by repeatedly saying, "We are all in the same canoe and must paddle together." Unfortunately, the HSTA, the AARP and others were not buying any appeals to shared sacrifice and fiscal responsibility. As they saw it, the budget was being balanced on their backs, not on the backs of everyone else. Also, in the middle of these initiatives, Gov. Abercrombie was recorded on a cell phone video (new at that time) where he was apparently taken by surprise and confronted in a public place by an angry constituent about the budget cuts. The man called him "Pal," and the governor angrily responded, "I'm not your pal. I'm the governor." Unfortunately, this video went viral and was widely played and replayed. As we all now know, YouTube videos seem to live forever.

The fiscal troubles of 2011 faded away as the national and local economies turned around, and within another year Gov. Abercrombie's conservative fiscal policies resulted in budget surpluses. However, the acrimony with the HSTA spanned several years and made Gov. Abercrombie unpopular in a number of different circles.

In my view, these hard fiscal choices were the major factor in costing Gov. Abercrombie a second term when he stood for reelection in 2014. George Will is credited with the saying, "If you're explaining, you're losing." There is never any good explanation that people are willing to hear when you are talking about raising their taxes or cutting their salaries. There are many politicians who simply kick the can down the road, failing to make the hard calls and leaving the problems for someone else. Gov. Abercrombie had the courage to try and deal with the fiscal problem. Unfortunately, those actions came back to haunt him in 2014, and he lost his primary bid for reelection. Because Hawai'i is a hugely Democratic state, the primary election is usually the only election that counts for governor. After David Ige won the general election to become governor, the HSTA got a giant collectively bargained contract pay raise.

In a larger sense, the problem of fiscal dilemmas for state governments has not gone away and has only gotten worse. The future unfunded fiscal liabilities of Hawai'i's state government loom as an unsustainable debt that eventually will have to be paid. The State provides pension benefits as well as health insurance benefits to retired state workers. The currently calculated future unfunded liabilities for pension benefits and health insurance costs for retirees are now approximately $26 billion, which is more than twice the annual state budget. Gov. Abercrombie and his successor, Gov. Ige, along with Kalbert Young, Wes Machida and other fiscally responsible budget and finance directors, successfully convinced the legislature to mandate that hundreds of millions of dollars be set aside each year to address these future liabilities.

However, this commitment has recently been suspended in light of fiscal problems created by the COVID-19 pandemic. It is unknown when things will return to the way they were. There are always financial pressures, and as government employees get raises each year, as well as increases in health benefits, such measures inexorably increase the potential liabilities associated with their future retirement and health benefits. How those future benefits will be paid for and whether the system is sustainable is a conundrum that has not been solved.

The Senator's Request

Sometimes things just sneak up and happen without warning. In December 2012, I got a call to come up to the governor's office. There was going to be a meeting with Jeff Watanabe and Walter A. Dods Jr., emissaries of Senator Daniel K. Inouye, and the governor wanted me to attend. Dods and Watanabe were ushered in, and we sat informally on the couches at one end of the large, spacious office, as if in a living room, rather than at the governor's desk. Perhaps this was as a sign of equals or a sign of respect, since these two were old lions of the Democratic Party in Hawai'i, part of the old guard. Dods was the CEO of First Hawaiian Bank, the largest bank in Hawai'i, and had been a kingmaker and counselor for many politicians for decades. He was a powerful person, someone who transcended the worlds of politics and business in Hawai'i. He had been a confidant of Senator Inouye and in his inner circle for many years. Watanabe was of similar stature. A leading lawyer and dealmaker in the community, he was an affable, relaxed man, with a smooth and personable manner. Watanabe was the senator's personal lawyer and consigliere. He had advised the senator on many occasions, both politically and when Senator Inouye faced some legal scandals for accusations of sexual harassment brought by his hairdresser.

It had been known for some time that the senator was having serious health problems. There had been stories in the paper noting that his health was deteriorating, that he only had one functioning lung, that he was not well. Dan Inouye was the most powerful politician in Hawaiʻi. He had been a stalwart of the Democratic Party for decades. He had a deep, stentorian voice, which he had used to good effect during the national Watergate committee hearings in Washington, when he asked the seminal questions, "What did the president know and when did he know it?" While the senator was known to be in poor health, it was not publicly known that he was in fact dying, a fact only known to insiders. The story had been carefully managed by his office, so that the press was not speculating, perhaps out of respect for the senator.

In the meeting that day were the governor; chief of staff Bruce Coppa; Marvin Wong, the governor's political advisor; and me, as the attorney general. We made some small talk. The governor, Dods and Watanabe had known each other for decades. Then Watanabe brought out an envelope and handed it to the governor, saying that they had just been in Washington, DC, had met with Senator Inouye and had a letter for the governor from the senator. Inouye wanted to ask a small favor of the governor, a personal request of a dying man. The governor took the envelope, opened it and read it silently to himself.

The senator wanted the governor to appoint US House Representative Colleen Hanabusa to his open Senate seat upon his death. Would he do so? The governor said he would consider the request. There was not much more to say. After a few pleasantries, Dods and Watanabe left.

After due consideration of this request, Gov. Abercrombie appointed his lieutenant governor, Brian Schatz, who was young, personable, intelligent and an experienced state politician, to succeed the senator. I thought the governor's decision was the right one, and I supported it. Senator Schatz was an up-and-coming politician who would be around for decades. As had been shown by Senator Inouye's career, it was important to amass seniority in the Senate, in order to rise in the ranks and have influence and power. Schatz represented the future. On the other hand, Representative Hanabusa was in her sixties and despite her greater experience could only serve in the Senate for a few terms at most, not long enough to amass significant seniority or power. I agreed with the governor's assessment that Schatz would serve the long-term interests of Hawai'i better.

Dods wrote in his autobiographical book, *Yes! A Memoir of Modern Hawaii*, that this was a pivotal moment, and that the refusal of Gov. Abercrombie to honor this request led to the governor's political downfall and loss in the next primary election. Dods's thinking was that this did not honor the legacy of the senator, and thus alienated the still very strong Japanese American community in Hawai'i. My own view is that although this meeting was a momentous occasion, it was not the major factor to cause the political downfall of the governor. The governor's failed reelection bid two years later was a culmination of dissatisfaction of various groups, and I don't believe the Japanese American community had the refused request of the senator primarily on its mind. Gov. Abercrombie had enjoyed great relations and support from the Japanese American community for many decades. The fact that David Ige was Japanese American gave him an advantage with this constituency, but not because of the refusal of the senator's request.

In the special election held a year and a half later, Senator Schatz beat Representative Hanabusa is an extremely close contest by only 1,700 votes. The fact that Schatz won this election led me to believe that the meeting with Dods and Watanabe was not the pivotal factor that caused the governor to be denied a second term.

I thought the meeting was interesting, as the official act of one king to another, as a communication of one powerful figure to another. It was also the long reach of the hand from the grave, as the old guard, embodied by the senator's letter, sought to control and direct the affairs of those who were still living. I was pleased to be in the room where it was happening, just to participate and see how the old lions conducted themselves.

The Day the Music Died

After Gov. Abercrombie's primary election loss in August 2014, it was fairly clear that I would have to move on. I had originally told the governor that I would commit to the position of attorney general for only four years, even if he won a second term, but I had grown to like the job. The opportunity to have a seat at the table and be in the room where things were happening was unparalleled and deeply satisfying. Keith Hiraoka, my former law partner, had been friends with governor-elect Ige from childhood days and was the campaign chair for his campaign. As I knew Hiraoka and had worked with Senator Ige for the past four years when he was chair of the Senate Ways and Means Committee, I naively held out some small hope that Gov. Ige might be interested in having me serve. I let Hiraoka know I was interested, but I just as quickly learned that Ige was not. I began thinking of what I would do, while also trying to wrap up various initiatives.

The National Association of Attorneys General was having its winter meeting in Florida at the beginning of December 2014, and I had been planning to go as a last hurrah to see my compatriots. NAAG asked me to speak on a panel, and so I found myself talking about some legal issue on Monday, December 4, 2014, at 4 p.m. Eastern Standard Time. The Hawai'i Constitution provides that the terms of the governor, and all department heads, including the attorney general, end at noon Hawai'i time on the first Monday of December following the new governor's election. When our presentation was over, at 5 p.m., because of the time difference, it was noon in Hawai'i, and I was no longer the attorney general. I happened to mention that fact in my panel talk.

On Tuesday morning, I went down to the NAAG sessions, and found that I had unceremoniously been demoted! The NAAG staff took me at my word and acted accordingly. On Monday I had been the attorney general of Hawai'i, with commensurate powers, a seat at the table with the other attorneys general, a nameplate and a microphone. The very next day I was just another guy. I no longer had a nameplate, a microphone or a seat at the table with the big boys. I was relegated to the back seats with the lobbyists and staffers. The music had stopped, and I was the guy without a chair. If I hadn't realized it before, this was a very public way of reminding me that the past four years had been all about the office, and not about me. An ignominious end. I could only laugh.

It was a sudden and quick denouement after four years of having an exhilarating, exciting and thoroughly enjoyable ride. I once had the opportunity, through the US Navy's Distinguished Visitor Embark Program, to go aboard the USS *Nimitz*, a nuclear-powered aircraft carrier, during Pacific Rim joint defense operations with twenty-plus other nations. It was amazing. We landed on the carrier deck and were caught by the tailhook. We watched almost round-the-clock operations of fighter jets (F14s and F22s) taking off and landing, day and night. When we left, we were launched off the carrier by the same steam catapult that launches the fighter jets. Zero to 165 mph in two seconds! What a ride! The g-forces were tremendous, the acceleration magnificent!

Becoming attorney general was much like getting shot off the *Nimitz* deck by steam catapult. One minute you're sitting in your chair minding your own business, and then suddenly you're flying at jet airspeed as you swear to protect the constitution and serve the State. It was all a tremendously fast ride and took me to heights that I had never thought I would see. This job was the ride of my life, the best job I ever had and the most fun and responsibility in any legal job I've had.

The end of my term as attorney general was just the opposite—it was like being caught by the tailhook. One moment you're flying along at high speed and the next moment you're jerked to a complete stop. That is exactly what it felt like. Sadly, my ride was over. ❦

| 14 |

Reflections on the Journey

My experience as attorney general was the opportunity of a lifetime. Reflecting on the experience, there were some lessons I learned along the way that I would like to share, in the hope that others can take from my experience and use it for their own goals and, I hope, the public interest.

What I Learned about Government

I have always believed that government can and should be an institution to improve the lives of people and allow them to live in harmony and should strive to do the greatest good for the greatest number. Government, with all of its resources and all of its power, can be a tremendous force for good, achievement and positive action. Of course, the devil is always in the details, and putting those ideals into practice and action is no small matter.

In my brief time serving as attorney general, I learned that our democratic system of government works. It's certainly not perfect, but it allowed us to address some major problems and accomplish significant achievements in dealing with the national mortgage foreclosure crisis, Native Hawaiian claims and environmental protections. We were able to make things better and improve the lives of people. Many people take our system of government for granted and love to blame government and political leaders, without thinking about how hard collective organization and action are, especially when there are large differences of opinion in what and how things should be done.

In my view, the reason we have such a tremendous system is because of the ideals of the Constitution and the fact that we have established a fair process for balancing and sharing power among different actors, branches of government and factions, while respecting peaceful dissent and opposing points of view. Our system allows for disagreement so that good ideas can come forward and attempt to win support in the marketplace of ideas. Most importantly, we have institutionalized a process for a peaceful periodic transfer of power, based on free and fair elections, to allow people to make their voices heard and affect the balance of power.

I learned that government is the best vehicle for solving big problems to ensure our collective future. In today's world, the size of the problems that confront us are so large that joint concerted action is the only way to address them. Solving large-scale interconnected problems such as economic recessions, disaster recovery, health pandemics, social justice issues and environmental issues requires significant thought, commitment and resources. Only government has the capacity, resources and authority to marshal and deploy the necessary measures to address such difficult and massive problems.

There truly are no viable alternatives to government action when our communities are confronted with huge problems. The Ronald Reagan idea of trying to downsize to "small" government is simply wrong, since it ignores the interconnectedness of our communities and the size of the problems we face. We will not solve massive problems by trying to put blinders on to harken back to a mythical vision of small-town government from a different age. Big problems demand big solutions.

The private sector and business community cannot solve major societal problems. They can help and they can support, but they cannot lead. Business interests have too narrow a focus on their own interests to focus on what is best for communities. One of the most pernicious developments in the last several decades has been the emergence of a dominant philosophy that businesses are supposed to be laser focused only upon making profits for their shareholders. The result has been a "me first" attitude that emphasizes what is good for narrow special interests, not our communities as a whole. This philosophy ignores the reality that businesses do not exist in a vacuum, that they can only succeed within the context of the communities they serve and are dependent upon a host of others, such as vendors, suppliers, employees and customers, for their success.

The big problems that our communities face, such as economic recession, health pandemics, climate change and social inequality, are simply too large, and businesses are too fractured and small to effectively deal with such problems. Few businesses have the resources, leadership, organization or desire to provide comprehensive solutions to large problems. For example, it was the big banks and mortgage companies that caused the mortgage foreclosure crisis and resulting Great Recession, precisely because of their narrow focus on what was best for each of them. Only government could act to solve that crisis in a timely fashion, forcing banks and mortgage companies to support solutions with the threat of litigation and liability.

Similar to economic problems, large-scale social justice problems require government leadership, since the private sector is reluctant to lead, as many of the issues are too political, too uncertain, too emotional and could have a negative impact on their businesses. Even enlightened business leaders cannot ignore their own business needs and imperatives to undertake the necessary missions that governments can.

The lessons I learned in my time in government have been reinforced and underscored by the events of the last four years. Our system of government and our capacity to address and solve large-scale societal and community problems have been under a relentless and systemic attack by President Donald Trump during this time. Trump actively attempted to dismantle the system and the process, and to create disrespect for the institutions of government and society. He lied repeatedly and had no respect for facts, simply making up "alternative facts" to serve his own interests. He had no respect for others with opposing viewpoints and celebrated those with discredited conspiracy theories and racist attitudes as being "very fine people." In perhaps his worst moment, on January 6, 2021, he made baseless, untrue claims that the 2020 presidential election had been stolen and fomented insurrection by inciting a mob of his followers to make a violent attack on Congress at the US Capitol to stop the election results from being confirmed.

Fortunately, Trump lost the 2020 presidential election to Joseph R. Biden, and his insurrection attempt and lies have been unsuccessful. There were many conservative Republicans who disavowed Trump and supported President Biden in the election. However, the fact that Trump received as many votes as he did and has continued to garner support from his right-wing base shows how fragile the institution of democracy in America is. When leaders such as Trump veer away from the institutional processes of a fair system of government and into hate, authoritarianism, lying and the encouragement of violence, our system of government and our society suffer.

I believe that the United States and the American people are better than that, better than the vision that Trump tried to sell to the nation. Based on my experiences, I believe that the American people, like the people of Hawai'i, are kind, decent and responsible, with great heart and compassion. We are people who share the same values of community, respect for others, fairness and equity. We are people who have more in common than the differences that may exist among us. We are better than the old hatreds, prejudices and fears that have been Trump's stock in trade.

In my experience, most people just want the same things—housing, education, prosperity for them and their children, acceptance, understanding, community, and the opportunity to work hard and succeed and not be limited by the color of their skin, or gender, or sexual orientation. Many people also want to make a difference, to be part of a solution and bigger mission, to be a positive force in the world.

When we look to our better angels, when we uphold and put into practice the ideals of the United States Constitution, of equality and opportunity, we enhance our collective future together. Hawai'i is an example of how races can live together in harmony, with a shared future, with cooperation, communication and life together, even on a few islands where there is nowhere else to go. The world is a global village, so we all have to succeed or fail together. It cannot be a zero-sum game of winners and losers. We are better than those who would seek to divide us and drive us apart.

In this regard, civic engagement and civic education are critically important for our communities and our young people. Democracy is fragile. It takes work to make sure that the people who vote understand what is at stake and how our government operates. Modern technology and communication on the Internet have accelerated the trends that fracture our shared consciousness, making it easy for us to retreat to silos and bubbles where we only hear what we want to hear. Without civic engagement and education, those trends will continue with alarming and negative effect, and the people in our communities will lose sight of the larger picture of living and working together for a better future.

I suppose that this may sound corny, but it is what I learned from my time in government. It is sometimes fashionable to be a skeptic, to question and denigrate civic virtues, somehow thinking that those are unsophisticated concepts not suited for today's world. I believe that is flat-out wrong. The basic principles we have always taught our children about our system of government are tried and true. The Gettysburg Address, the Pledge of Allegiance and the Declaration of Independence have not lost their meaning or vitality.

What I Learned about Accomplishing Goals in Government

Governing is hard. It is not for the faint of heart, as it requires courage, leadership and willpower to try and accomplish things for the common good. Because there is so much money and power associated with many government processes, there are many interests that seek to bend the arc of government action to their benefit. People are people, and there are always those who seek to use government for their own ends, not necessarily those of the common good. There are a number of factors unique to government that influence the ability of governmental leaders to achieve goals.

First, politics and election cycles are overriding factors that confront public sector leaders. Government institutions are ultimately subject to politics and democracy, a process that requires the consent of the governed in regular elections. Sometimes, important but controversial issues cannot be pushed forward when there are upcoming elections, because politicians are concerned about being reelected. Providing the political will to solve long-standing problems is neither easy nor simple, and the problems that remain are thorny and difficult. One structural issue is that the four-year political cycle is sometimes not long enough for difficult problems to be properly addressed and solved. Even eight years for a governor's administration is barely enough to address difficult problems.

Second, the importance and influence of the media and social media cannot be overstated. The free flow of information through media and social media avenues clearly impacts decision-making by government institutions and leaders. Media coverage can influence public perception on various issues. Social media coverage can be more unfiltered and wilder than media coverage, but just as effective, and sometimes more effective. Sometimes, because of space or time limitations or the intent of reporters, complex issues can be reduced to slogans and simplistic formulations that confuse or distort the issue and hamper reasoned decision-making. Media and social media coverage can certainly bring attention to issues. At the same time, clear and honest communication through both is critical to making sure the electorate is aware of and understands what is happening in government.

Third, the processes of public sector decision-making in the executive, legislative and regulatory environments are critical, but sometimes unknown or misunderstood. Many people who are not familiar with government think that government processes are a black box, which cannot be deciphered without knowing the secret handshake. Actually, government processes are usually governed by statutes, rules, tradition and inertia. Such processes have their own internal logic and gatekeepers. Timing can be everything. Because the process of legislation or administrative regulation is complicated, knowing the rules can be the critical difference between successfully accomplishing policy objectives and having initiatives derailed by adversaries.

Fourth, special interests are often involved in trying to shape and direct what government does. Government is supposed to be concerned with the public interest, rather than special interests. Special interests are not necessarily bad if they also serve the public interest. Thus, special interests will try to show that their interests align with the public interest. Public sector leaders must be clear-eyed about the effects of special interests and money, how the public interest may be affected, and wary that public initiatives are not hijacked or subverted by special interests. Special interests bring money to the table for political actors. The reality is that it can cost millions of dollars to run even a modest political campaign in our modern world. Disclosures of special interest money are critical. Where the money comes from and how it affects decisions are important issues that government and the electorate must always be prepared to deal with.

All of these factors can affect and constrain the exercise of power and authority to accomplish goals. In his recent book, *The End of Power*, Moises Naim writes that, "in the 21st century, power is easier to get, harder to use—and easier to lose." Naim describes how governments are increasingly restricted from the exercise of power through traditional leaders and institutions, as recent developments in the flow of information, social media and protests have made political and corporate leadership vulnerable to challenges from smaller, more nimble adversaries. Naim puts forth the provocative argument that societies are becoming both increasingly constrained and more anarchic, since smaller actors now have the power to veto but not dictate, i.e., destroy but not create, thus creating gridlock, anarchy, or both. Naim's thesis is a cautionary warning to all who want to achieve goals in the public sector.

What I Learned about Leadership

I have been asked what advice I would give to young people, or to a younger me, about leadership, in light of my experience. For those who might be interested, I offer the following thoughts.

First, consider stepping up to serve and be a leader. Leadership is the single most important factor for the world and our communities. As our global village continues to become more and more interdependent, the leaders that our communities have will determine our futures, whether good or bad. They will determine whether we will solve critical problems, create a better world, succeed or fail. The caliber of leaders in our institutions will affect whether we can adapt to change, make progress and achieve positive outcomes.

Leadership provides direction, meaning and purpose to people. Leaders provide critical analysis and decision-making to accomplish goals and solve problems. In a world of uncertainty and indecision, they hopefully will provide integrity, focus and responsibility for groups of people. Our communities need leaders to help guide them along. Consider serving in government or for nonprofits. These are noble pursuits, as both seek to improve all of our lives for the common good.

Second, apply yourself and learn the many different and varied skills of leadership. You will not go wrong. In today's world, the more skills you have, the better. There are many books and courses about the characteristics and skills of leaders. Read them. Learn about character, trust, communication, people skills, emotional intelligence, management skills, writing skills and executive decision-making. Practice such skills by serving in nonprofit organizations. Nonprofits can provide valuable experience in participation and decision-making that might not otherwise be available to a young person.

There are two skills that I consider of paramount importance. One of those is communication. Learn to express yourself clearly, both verbally and in writing. Learn to communicate your thoughts to create passion and excitement. Communication is also a two-way street. The best communicators are also great listeners. Learn to put yourself in the other person's shoes and actively listen to others to understand their concerns, anxieties and motivations, so that you can speak to their concerns. Learn negotiation skills—the ability to understand the positions and interests of others in order to find shared interests and values that can lead to common solutions. Since people do things for their reasons, not yours, a leader must be able to understand and communicate both his or her own reasons and the reasons of others to find common ground for accomplishment.

The other skill of a leader I consider important is understanding the perspective of the group. General Omar Bradley, the first chairman of the Joint Chiefs of Staff, said, "The greatness of a leader is measured by the achievements of the led. This is the ultimate test of his effectiveness." The role of the leader is to get the team, the organization, the community to achieve a goal, not to achieve personal glory. It is the difference between being a mountain climber and a mountain climbing guide. The mountain climber is focused on her individual achievement in reaching the summit of the mountain. The mountain climbing guide, on the other hand, is focused on having the entire team reach the summit together. An effective leader will emphasize the achievements of the group, as opposed to his individual achievements. The role of the leader is to work for those who work for him.

Third, put yourself out there and volunteer. Don't wait to be asked. Good things will come of it. If you have an interest in something, let others who have similar interests know, and ask how you can help. My friend John Radcliffe, a veteran union leader, educator and political lobbyist, told me once about how he ran for state office. He did not win, but people appreciated that he was willing to put himself on the line and step up, and good opportunities came to him as a result. My experience has been the same. I have succeeded through the kindness of friends and strangers who have assisted me and have let me know they appreciated that I stepped up to take on a particular role. One role led to another and another and together they got me to where I am today. Of course, you should not expect to reap rewards from your volunteer service. They may or may not come. But the intrinsic value to yourself and to those around you of serving and learning from such service is priceless.

Fourth, when someone asks for your help and you decide to give it, do something as quickly as you can. Senior US district judge Charles R. Breyer, the brother of US Supreme Court justice Stephen G. Breyer, once told me a story about a legendary lawyer in California, who was an old-school confidant of highly placed political and business figures. Part of this lawyer's success was that he kept in his shirt pocket a small notebook of requests for favors and would act as quickly as he could whenever he got a request, then cross it off in his notebook. His reasoning was that if he was able to get a result quickly, the person for whom he got that result would be extremely grateful and would hold him in high regard for being a magician. Even if no positive result was forthcoming, the person would be very grateful when he learned that the lawyer had acted so promptly, even just to try. But if nothing was done for a while, or if the person had to ask again, then the curve of gratitude would drop off rapidly, and he or she wouldn't be as grateful, even if a positive result were to occur later. It was the speed of action that showed that the person was held in high regard, and that high regard would usually be reciprocated and paid back in spades. I have found the same result in my experience. People are very appreciative that you have tried to assist them and have not delayed or waited to do so.

Fifth, remember that time is a very fleeting commodity. You may think you have a lot of time to accomplish your goals, but time slips away a lot faster than we think. It certainly did for me. Four years may seem like a long time, but my term in office went by really fast. To accomplish meaningful and lasting goals is hard work that requires substantial time, time to work with and convince others to agree, time to comply with existing procedures, time to deal with all of the details and unforeseen complications attendant to doing something important. Apply yourself diligently, because the time will never be enough.

Finally, always remember the human dimensions and the people aspects of whatever you are involved in. One of the key things I've learned from my time as a lawyer and attorney general is that it is important for us to always focus on the human consequences of the problems at hand. The issues that came to us, the policies and procedures we opined on, the agency decisions that were made, were not just some ethereal hypothetical constructs, but instead dealt with real people, their lives, fortunes, hopes and dreams, and had real consequences to them.

As attorney general it was critical for me to take into account the human consequences of any decisions or actions and always think about the larger picture—whether we were doing the right thing for the most people. Even when we had to say no or enforce a policy that adversely affected others, we needed to be able to consider the consequences to people's lives. Without such empathy, you will not be able to fully appreciate the concerns of all involved to try and fashion the right solution. I have found that after all is said and done, it is the people who make important things worth doing.

At the End of the Day

Serving as attorney general really was immensely meaningful and satisfying. I used the time, tools and resources available to address and try to solve problems, to make things better. What I remember most was the overall sense of purpose, that each day I was contributing to a larger goal and helping people. I tried to get as much done as I could, knowing that whether I was involved in big or small matters, my efforts would contribute to the tapestry of government action that was being woven daily, that my story would be part of the fabric of history and society, building on the accomplishments of those who came before me and providing a foundation for those who would come later. I am forever grateful that I was allowed to serve. ❦

ACKNOWLEDGMENTS

I owe a debt of gratitude to Paul and Emma Louie, my father and mother, that can never properly be repaid. They provided so much love, guidance, support and caring and helped me to make my way through the world and achieve whatever success I have been able to garner. They provided me with unstinting examples of hard work and perseverance, along with a moral compass and a strong sense of right and wrong, which set me on the path to where I am today. Johanna, my wife, has been a loving and strongly supportive partner for all that I have achieved and enjoyed in life. Ryan and Jenna, my son and daughter, have achieved much and been a great joy to me as they have grown and blossomed.

Serving as attorney general of Hawai'i was for me both a serendipitous opportunity and a tremendous endeavor. Writing a book about the experience and what I learned was no easy task. I could not have done either without the encouragement and assistance of so many people who helped me along the way.

I am forever grateful to Gov. Neil Abercrombie for putting his faith and trust in me to be his attorney general and for his leadership of Hawai'i. Bill Kaneko and Kate Stanley have my undying gratitude for encouraging me to put my hat in the ring for the position, and for helping me navigate the job in so many ways. Alan Oshima gave me some great advice that set my mind at ease to pursue this job. Working with the governor and his team to move Hawai'i forward was a rare and fulfilling privilege. Bruce Coppa, the governor's chief of staff; Blake Oshiro, the deputy chief of staff; and Kalbert Young, the budget and finance director, were a joy to work with, as they were and are first-rate political and governmental strategists who did a lot for Hawai'i and taught me a lot about how government works.

I am indebted to so many people at the Department of the Attorney General, who counseled and advised me on how to successfully do the job, and then helped to execute all of the things we needed to do. Charleen Aina was a senior deputy with wide-ranging knowledge of the department, who served like a general minister without portfolio, giving me insight into the department as well as the many legal and political issues confronting the state. Charleen was particularly helpful in addressing Native Hawaiian issues. Russell Suzuki was another senior deputy with broad experience who served ably as first deputy attorney general, helping to keep the trains of the department running on time. A special shout-out is due to my dear departed friend Harvey Henderson, whom I brought into the department as a special major litigation supervisor, and who helped handle many of the big and complex litigation cases confronting the state.

I could not have done the job without the assistance of the executive team inside the Office of the Attorney General, the members of which I worked with on a daily basis. Josh Wisch was my executive special assistant for the first two years and helped me with all types of special projects that needed attention. Anne Lopez served in the same position for the last two years and became a great friend and confidante. Both Josh and Anne provided counsel, strategic thinking, friendship and humor to get the job done. David Moore handled the department's $70 million annual budget and was a master at understanding the State's finances and finding money when we needed it. Ann Nishihira, my secretary, and Jan Hasegawa, Russell's and Josh's secretary, made the place hum by getting the work out and interfacing with the rest of the department. Everyone in OAG worked well together and made the job fun, despite the pressures.

I am also very thankful for the assistance of the many supervisors and deputies who worked with me to carry out the many missions of the department. Supervisors Heidi Rian, Hugh Jones, Diane Taira, Frances Lum, Donna Kalama, Bill Wynhoff, Holly Shikada, Jim Halvorson, Diane Erickson, Pat Ohara, Girard Lau, Maurice Kato, Michael Vincent, Chris Young, Liane Moriyama, Julie Ebato, Marie Gavigan and Karen Inagaki all helped keep the department on track and moving, providing me with the necessary understanding of issues as they arose, and providing legal advice, counsel and representation to our many, many State clients.

Special thanks goes to deputies Jill Nagamine, James Walther and Anne Lopez, who provided important assistance for the same-sex marriage issues we addressed. There were many other line deputies who took care of important matters too numerous to list. I could not have done the job without all of them.

I very much enjoyed the camaraderie, friendship and opportunity to work together with the many state attorneys general I served with at the national level. There are far too many to try to list them all, but my thanks go to those I really connected with—Dustin McDaniel, Doug Gansler, Martha Coakley, Ellen Rosenblum, Catherine Cortez-Masto, Karl Racine, Jack Conway, Jim Hood, William Sorrell, Bob Ferguson, Bob Cooper, Lawrence Wasden, Marty Jackley, Lenny Rapadas, and Sam Olens—as well as past attorneys general Patrick Lynch and Terry Goddard. I also want to thank Karen White, the executive director of the Conference of Western Attorneys General and the Attorney General Alliance, for all of her help and support.

I'm indebted to my partners and friends at Roeca Louie & Hiraoka, where I found success as a lawyer for twenty-two years before leaving for government service. Art Roeca, Keith Hiraoka, April Luria and James Shin were great partners and friends, as well as wonderful lawyers. We had fun working up cases and trying lawsuits. Colleen Izutsu, my steadfast and terrific litigation secretary, kept my practice organized and humming along. May she rest in peace.

I'm exceptionally thankful for the many Asian American attorneys whom I met in law school, in practice and through the National Asian Pacific American Bar Association, and who have been great friends and colleagues over many decades. To name just a few: United States senator Mazie Hirono, Dale Minami, Don Tamaki, Ed Chen, the late Edwin Lee, Colbert Matsumoto, Hoyt Zia, Leigh-Ann Miyasato, Eric Yamamoto, Louise Ing, Charlene Shimada, Debbie Ching, Gene Lam, Bill Kaneko, Leighton Oshima, Vincent Eng, John Yang, Brian Sun, Sid Kanazawa, Paul Hirose, Bruce Ishimatsu, Wendy Shiba and Judy Lam. They have kept me grounded and abreast of social justice issues in the Asian American community for many years.

Making this book project a reality was more difficult than I had imagined. But the encouragement and help I received from many quarters helped get this to the finish line, and going through the process was very rewarding. Robin Hensley helped to convince me to take on this endeavor. A special thanks to Colin Moore, the best political media commentator in Hawai'i, who spent countless hours talking with me, helping me refine my thinking and guiding me in turning rough thoughts into clearer concepts. I'm especially grateful to my friends Hoyt Zia, Colbert Matsumoto, Dale Minami, Bill Kaneko, Frances Lum, Jonathan Moore, Louise Ing, Alan Van Etten and Leslie Hayashi, who took their valuable time to read my manuscript, give me cogent feedback and let me know when certain aspects were not ready for prime time. Stephen Louie, my brother; Jenna Louie, my daughter; and Frances Lum provided very valuable, substantial and critical discussions, editing and reframing, along with detailed and frank comments that helped me get this manuscript into suitable shape.

In my experience, for all successful endeavors of any substantive nature, it takes the sustained and collective efforts of many people. My service as attorney general and this book project are no different. I have been the beneficiary of the kindness, assistance and hard work of many friends, colleagues and strangers. My apologies to those I may have forgotten to thank. Without the selfless contributions of so many people, I would not be where I am today. My grateful thanks to all. ❦

INDEX

H

I

J

K

L

M

N

O

P

R

S

T

V

W

Y

Z

ABOUT THE AUTHOR

SEAN MARRS

David M. Louie is a civil trial lawyer at Kobayashi Sugita & Goda, LLP in Honolulu, Hawaiʻi—handling complex commercial litigation, construction defect claims, catastrophic personal injury defense, constitutional issues for the State of Hawaiʻi, government affairs, and lobbying—and also serves as a mediator and arbitrator. He was Hawaiʻi's attorney general from 2011 to 2014, providing advice, counsel and representation to the governor, cabinet, legislature, State agencies and employees. He has served as president, vice president and director of the Hawaiʻi State Bar Association, as Lawyer Representative for the Ninth Circuit Court of Appeals, and as Northwest Regional Governor for the National Asian-Pacific American Bar Association. He graduated from Occidental College and Berkeley Law School and currently lives in Honolulu.